Royal Conservatory of Music
GUITAR SERIES

REPERTOIRE AND STUDIES

Grade 1
Grade 2
Grade 3
Grade 4
Grade 5
Grade 6
Grade 7
Grade 8

SCALES AND ARPEGGIOS

Grades 1 through 10

The Frederick Harris Music Co., Limited
(416) 845-3487
Printed in Canada

529 S, ᵊers Road, Oakville, Ontario,
Canac ᵓ2G4
Imprim. ᵕu Canada

1990

ROYAL CONSERVATORY · OF MUSIC · TORONTO
18 86
EDITION

Syllabus

GUITAR

© *Copyright 1990 by The Frederick Harris Music Co., Limited*
All Rights Reserved

ISBN 0-88797-337-X

Official Examination Syllabus of the
Royal Conservatory of Music
Grades 1 through ARCT

Syllabus officiel des examens du
Royal Conservatory of Music
Niveau 1 jusqu'au ARCT

This 1990-edition Guitar Syllabus replaces all previous issues and is effective until further notice.

ANNUAL APPLICATION CLOSING DATES

Summer—March 1
Winter—November 1

Applications received after the closing dates cannot be accepted.
PLEASE MAIL EARLY

EXAMINATION FEES

Refer to the current Schedule of Examination Fees sheet available upon request.

NORTH AMERICAN EXAMINATION SCHEDULE

Practical

Winter:
Last three weeks of January
Summer:
Last two weeks of May and all of June
Monday - Saturday:
9:00 a.m. to 6:00 p.m.

Theory

Winter:
Second Friday and immediately following Saturday in December
Summer:
Second Friday and immediately following Saturday in May

Friday:
9:30 a.m. to 12:30 p.m.
Teacher's Written ARCT
9:30 a.m. to 12:30 p.m.
Counterpoint 4
9:30 a.m. to 12:30 p.m.
Comprehensive Theory
2:00 p.m. to 5:00 p.m.
History 3, 4, and 5

Saturday:
9:30 a.m. to 12:30 p.m.
Harmony 3, 4, and 5
9:30 a.m. to 11:30 a.m.
Rudiments 1
9:30 a.m. to 10:30 a.m.
Preliminary Rudiments
2:00 p.m. to 5:00 p.m.
Analysis 5
2:00 p.m. to 4:00 p.m.
Rudiments 2

APPLICATION ADDRESS

"Applications," Examination Department
Royal Conservatory of Music
273 Bloor Street West,
Toronto, Ontario,
M5S 1W2
(416) 978-3765
FAX (416) 978-3853

1990 ROYAL CONSERVATORY OF MUSIC TORONTO 1886 EDITION

Syllabus

GUITAR

TABLE OF CONTENTS

Each year, the Royal Conservatory of Music, in association with thousands of dedicated teachers across Canada and around the world, assists in the education of more than a quarter of a million students. The Conservatory's curriculum and examination system are built on a century of commitment to excellence in the teaching and performing of music. That commitment continues.

The Toronto Conservatory of Music opened in September 1887 with an enrolment of 200 students and a staff of fifty teachers. Edward Fisher was the founder and first Music Director of the new school, which occupied two floors above a music store at the corner of Yonge Street and Wilton Avenue. Through its professional training, national examination system, and faculty of distinguished musicians, the Conservatory quickly established itself as the dominant music training force in Canada, and subsequently one of the most significant musical institutions in the Commonwealth. In just ten years' time, when enrolment had grown to over 1000 students, the school was moved into newly built facilities which included a reception hall, offices, studios, classrooms, a lecture hall, and a concert hall. Additional studios, classrooms, and residences for out-of-town students were added over the next fifteen years. The Conservatory established its first local examination centres in several Ontario towns and opened branches in residential areas of Toronto in 1898. Augustus Vogt, conductor of the Toronto Mendelssohn Choir, became Principal following the death of Edward Fisher. In association with Sir Edmund Walker, President of the Conservatory, Vogt established closer ties with the University of Toronto, and in 1921 the operation passed to the University for administration by a Board of Trustees. Under the leadership of Principal Vogt and Sir Edmund Walker, new programs were developed, the number of examination centres was increased, and enrolment continued to grow, reaching nearly 7,500 in 1926, a year in which more than 16,000 candidates took examinations. Ernest MacMillan was named Principal in 1926. Through his efforts, the library was expanded and new courses, including opera classes, were introduced. The Conservatory's profile in the community was actively promoted through concert appearances of students and faculty. An annual Summer School Program was developed which continues to offer courses for performers, teachers, and children to the present day. When Sir Ernest MacMillan resigned in 1942, the leadership of the Conservatory passed in turn to Norman Wilks, Charles Peaker, and Ettore Mazzoleni, who served as Principal for twenty-three years following his appointment in 1945. A Royal Charter was granted to the Toronto Conservatory of Music by King George VI on 1 August 1947 in recognition of its wide influence. The Conservatory continued to develop under the leadership of distinguished musicians: Edward Johnson, Chairman of the Board of Trustees from 1947 to 1959, Ettore Mazzoleni, Principal, Arnold Walter, Director of the Senior School, and Boyd Neel, who served as Dean from 1953 to 1971. This important phase of its history saw the implementation of professional performance training programs offered through the Senior School, including the Artist Diploma Program and the Royal Conservatory Opera School, which provided training in all aspects of opera production. Dr. David Ouchterlony became Principal in 1968. In 1978 he was succeeded by Gordon Kushner, who served as Acting Principal until the appointment of Ezra Schabas as Principal later that year. Gustav Ciamaga, Dean of the Faculty of Music, University of Toronto, was appointed Acting Principal in July 1983 and was succeeded in 1984 by Robert Dodson, who was appointed Principal in January 1987. He was succeeded by Gordon Kushner, who in August 1988 became Acting Principal for a second time.

In June 1984, a report from a University of Toronto Provostial Task Force recommended that the Royal Conservatory of Music separate from the University. On 10 February 1987, as the process of becoming independent from the University of Toronto was under way, the Royal Conservatory of Music celebrated the commencement of its second century with an historic gala Centennial Benefit Concert in Roy Thomson Hall, which featured distinguished alumni including Lois Marshall, Steven Staryk, and Jon Vickers, and was broadcast on national radio and television. The proceeds from this concert were contributed to a scholarship endowment fund.

As it begins its second century, and in anticipation of the future needs of the Canadian and international music communities, the Royal Conservatory of Music has strengthened its General Studies and Ensembles and Chamber Music programs and expanded its Professional Studies programs, offering students a broad range of full-time study options, including the Artist Diploma, Performance Diploma, Artist-Teacher, Resident ARCT, and Orchestral Training programs.

The Artist Diploma Program is a two-year course designed for students who demonstrate exceptional talent, artistic maturity and the potential to pursue a solo or chamber-music career. The curriculum includes two hours of private instruction per week in addition to monthly master classes given by internationally acclaimed performers. Artist Diploma students frequently give public recitals in and around Toronto.

The Performance Diploma program is designed to develop the performance potential of young musicians at the post-secondary level. Development of individual performance standards is the focus of this four-year program. Theory, history, humanities, and French language studies are required to ensure that each graduate is knowledgeable in a broad range of musical and general studies.

The Artist-Teacher program, recently introduced, addresses the needs of community musicians who must adapt and respond to a variety of musical challenges with performing, teaching, and entrepreneurial skills, and who can assume a leadership role in the musical life of their communities. The curriculum includes private instruction, chamber music, vocal and instrumental accompanying, pedagogy, theoretical subjects, improvisation, conducting, the use of new technologies, and administrative and marketing skills.

The Resident ARCT program was introduced in 1988. Available to post-secondary students who have reached a Grade 8 performance level, this course leads to the Associateship Diploma (Performer's or Teacher's) and includes weekly instruction in theory, ear training, history, minor instrument, pedagogy, and ensemble, in addition to intensive study on the principal instrument.

Orchestral musicians may prepare for careers in professional orchestras through the Orchestral Training program, introduced by the Royal Conservatory in 1979. Participants perform in the Royal Conservatory Orchestra which presents an annual concert series. Graduates have assumed positions in most major orchestras in Canada. The one-year course of study includes instruction in orchestral playing techniques, audition preparation, and chamber music, as well as sectional rehearsals and lessons.

With the enduring success of established Royal Conservatory of Music programs, the expansion of curricula for senior students and new initiatives such as the 1988 publication of the Centennial Celebration Series of piano repertoire and studies, the Royal Conservatory continues to serve the needs of thousands of musicians and music students in Canada, and an expanding constituency in the U.S.A., Europe and the Far East.

PART I

APPLICATIONS

The Royal Conservatory of Music welcomes applications from all interested individuals. Anyone may apply to be examined in practical or theoretical music subjects, with the limitation that some grade levels and subjects have a minimum age for applicants. Any teacher may submit students for examinations. Application forms and fee schedules are available at the main building or any branch of the Royal Conservatory of Music, from affiliated representatives and coordinators, and from local music stores. Please use a separate application for each practical and theoretical subject. Applications are accepted by the Royal Conservatory of Music on the understanding that Candidates will comply with the procedures and requirements outlined in the relevant Syllabus. Applications with accompanying fees — currently, payment is accepted by cheque or money order in Canadian dollars and by Mastercard or VISA — must be received by the Examination Department of the Royal Conservatory of Music on or before the closing dates, which are 1 March for the Summer Session and 1 November for the Winter Session. Faxed applications must be accompanied by your charge card number and expiry date. The Royal Conservatory of Music cannot be responsible for delays in delivery of the mail or for incomplete or incorrect applications. Applications must be mailed early in order to ensure their arrival on or before the closing date. Late applications will not be processed under any circumstances. PLEASE APPLY EARLY.

SCHEDULING AND FEE EXTENSIONS

Notification

A timetable giving the centre location, date, and time of examination will be mailed to each applicant following the closing date for applications. Please verify the correctness of the information on your notification and immediately inform the Examination Department of any errors. In the event of a conflict with school examinations, notify the local representative or coordinator. Every effort will be made to reconcile the schedules. Candidates can be rescheduled only by the Examination Department, and only at the discretion of the Department. Candidates may not trade times with other Candidates. Once received by the Examination Department, an application cannot be withdrawn. As a courtesy, please contact the Department or your local representative or coordinator if you plan not to attend your scheduled examination. Under very limited conditions, outlined below, extensions and partial refunds of fees are granted.

Extensions

Candidates who are unable to take an examination for medical reasons will be granted an extension of the full examination fee upon receipt of a physician's certificate within two weeks following the examination date. Alternatively, such Candidates may request a refund of half the examination fee. Candidates who are unable to take an examination because of an unresolvable academic conflict will be granted an extension of the fee upon receipt

of a letter from a school official a MINIMUM of two weeks BEFORE the examination date. Alternatively, the Candidate may request a refund of half the examination fee. Fee extensions will be valid for one year from the date of the scheduled examination. It is the responsibility of the student to reapply for examination within the period of eligibility.

Religious Observances

Candidates may request that their examinations not be scheduled on certain days for religious reasons. Such requests must be made at the time of application.

Results

Results of examinations in all subjects are mailed following the completion of examination sessions across Canada. Duplicate marks and transcripts are available from the Examination Department. Results are not given by telephone. Practical examination Candidates will receive the original report of the examiner. Theory examination Candidates will receive a breakdown of marks for each question on the examination. Please refer to the Theory Syllabus for procedures concerning the re-reading of theory examination papers. See the Table of Detailed Markings (p. 10) for further information on the grading of Guitar examinations.

CERTIFICATES

Certificates are awarded to successful Candidates twice annually (April and October). Commencing at the Grade 5 level, practical certificates will be issued upon the successful completion of the designated theory co-requisites within five years following the session of the initial practical examination. No time limit applies when theory co-requisites are taken prior to practical examinations. Please refer to the individual practical grades and the current Theory Syllabus for specific theory co-requisites. Separate certificates are awarded for each grade in theory upon successful completion of all requirements for the grade. Grade 10 certificates are awarded when minimum requirements have been completed whether or not prerequisites for the ARCT examination have been met. ARCT diplomas are awarded to Candidates at the annual November Convocation ceremony in Toronto or are forwarded immediately following Convocation. Candidates may not use the designation ARCT before Convocation.

MEDALS

Medals are awarded on the basis of examination results. No application is required. Candidates taking supplemental examinations or repeating examinations to upgrade marks are not eligible for medals or scholarships.

Gold Medals

Gold medals are awarded annually to ARCT Candidates who have obtained the highest practical marks in each of the following disciplines: piano, organ, accordion, strings, guitar, orchestral instruments (brass, woodwinds, and percussion), singing, and speech and drama. Candidates must obtain a minimum of 80 percent in the practical examination to qualify for the Gold Medal. All prescribed theory requirements must be completed prior to or at the same session as the practical examination with an average of at least 70 percent. In the case of a tie, the Candidates' past examination records will be considered. A Gold Medal will not be awarded in a discipline in which fewer than five Candidates have entered in a given year.

Silver Medals

Silver Medals are awarded annually (in Canada by province or region) to Candidates in Grades 1 to 10 who have obtained the highest marks in each grade and discipline including: piano, organ, accordion, strings, guitar, orchestral instruments (brass, woodwinds, and percussion) singing, and speech and drama. To qualify for these awards, Candidates must obtain at least 80 percent and must also have completed the prescribed theory requirements for their respective grades. In the case of a tie, the award will be given to the Candidate with the better past examination record. A Silver Medal will not be awarded in a grade and discipline for which fewer than five Candidates are entered in any province or region in a given year.

SECONDARY SCHOOL MUSIC CREDITS AND SCHOLARSHIPS

Candidates are advised to consult their school principal or guidance counsellor on the eligibility of Royal Conservatory of Music examinations for secondary school credit and university entrance. In Ontario, RCM examinations are accepted as credits toward Ontario secondary school graduation diplomas, and may be used in qualifying for Ontario Scholarships. For information on the current availability of examination scholarships for guitar Candidates, please contact the Examination Department.

PART II

PROCEDURES AND REGULATIONS

1 **Syllabus List Substitutions**

Candidates for practical examinations in Grades 1-10 may substitute, without prior approval, one piece from the corresponding list from the next higher grade, played EXACTLY as listed. A Grade 8 List C or D piece will be accepted for Grade 7 List C; a Grade 10 List D or E piece will be accepted for Grade 9 List D. Studies may not be substituted.

2 **Irregular List Requests**

All candidates for practical examinations may request approval to play one piece not listed in this Syllabus according to the following outline:

Grade 1 . . . . Any List
Grade 2 . . . . List A or B
Grades 3-7 . . . . List A, B, or C
Grade 8 . . . . List A, B, C, or D
Grades 9-ARCT . . . . List A, B, or C

Requests for approval must be submitted on the official Irregular List Form available from the Examination Department and must reach the Examination Department no later than the closing dates for applications. The following policies apply to Irregular List applications. In addition to the piece submitted for approval, candidates must indicate on the Irregular List Form all other pieces to be performed at the examination. A copy of the irregular piece must be submitted with the Irregular List Form and will be returned to the applicant with official notification. Approval will be based upon the suitability of the level of difficulty and style of the submitted piece. Five (5) marks will be deducted from the final examination mark for the use of an unapproved piece. An approved Irregular List form must be handed to the examiner. All applications for approval of an irregular list must be accompanied by a fee. Contact the Examination Department for the current fee.

3 **Own Choice**

A candidate may substitute without special approval one selection of equal difficulty and musical quality not listed in the Syllabus in the following grades: Grade 9, List D; Grade 10, List D or E; ARCT (Performer's or Teacher's), List D or E. The substituted selection must be of the same period as the works in the list in which the substitution is being made. Judgment shown in selecting an Own Choice substitution will be considered in the marking. For this reason, the Royal Conservatory of Music will not answer questions or give advice on the suitability of substitutions. Candidates should clearly indicate such a substitution as OWN CHOICE on the list of pieces handed to the examiner.

4 **Memory**

All technical tests must be played from memory. Studies need not be memorized, nor are extra marks awarded if studies are played from memory. In Grades 1 to 6, where memorization is marked separately, full marks for this aspect of the performance will be given for each piece satisfactorily memorized. Partial marks for memorization MAY be given, at the discretion of the examiner, even if the music is not entirely memorized. In Grades 7 to 10, candidates are expected to perform from memory. Marks are automatically deducted for failure to play from memory. However, candidates may elect not to memorize the music and the examination will still be graded, the final mark reflecting a significant penalty for failure to memorize. For Performer's and Teacher's ARCT, memorization is compulsory and candidates failing to perform from memory will receive no marks. The examiners will, however, provide written comments on any such unmemorized performance. Such performances do not qualify for examination awards or toward the ARCT diploma.

5 **Fingerings**

Any appropriate system of fingering will be accepted for repertoire, except where a particular edition is expressly required in the Syllabus (e.g., THIS EDITION ONLY). In such cases, the candidate must observe the fingering stipulated in the edition.

6 **Visually Impaired Candidates**

Special policies for visually impaired candidates may be obtained by writing to the Examination Department. Inquiries should be received no later than the closing date for applications: March 1 (Summer Session) and November 1 (Winter Session).

7 **Editions**

Any standard edition is acceptable unless expressly prohibited. Students are encouraged to use the best edition available, that is, the edition which best reflects the composer's intentions.

8 **Repeats and Da Capo**

In playing pieces and studies, repeat signs should not be observed except where specifically noted in official Royal Conservatory of Music publications. Da Capo signs must be observed.

9 **Interruptions**

At the examiner's discretion, the performance of pieces and studies may be interrupted when an assessment of the performance has been reached.

10 **Miscellaneous Information**

Warmup rooms are provided for guitar candidates. Candidates must be ready to perform ten minutes before the scheduled time. Candidate numbers on official timetables must not be changed. Pieces and studies to be performed must be listed on the reverse side of the timetable. Candidates must bring a legal copy of the music to the examination (photocopies not acceptable) whether or not the music is memorized. Only the examiner(s) and the candidate are permitted in the examination room except where the Syllabus permits or requires a piece to be accompanied. Accompanists are permitted in the examination room only for the duration of their accompanimental duties. Page turners and other assistants are not permitted. Designated waiting areas are provided for parents, teachers, accompanists, and other assistants. Handicapped students may receive assistance into and out of the examination room, but helpers must remain in the waiting area during the examination.

11 Centres

Royal Conservatory of Music examination centres are located throughout Canada. European candidates are examined in Lahr, West Germany, and a centre has been established in Hong Kong for candidates from the Far East. The establishment and maintenance of local examination centres depend upon demand and the availability of facilities. Please submit proposals for local centres to the Examination Department. ARCT Centres are centres which include Grade 10 and ARCT examinations. Candidates may apply at Winter sessions on the understanding that the examination may be deferred to the next session or transferred to the nearest ARCT Centre if the number of candidates is insufficient to warrant a specialist examination. A Private Centre for practical examinations may be requested where the number of candidates is insufficient to permit a regular centre. The Examination Department reserves the right to decline requests. Local participants must assume the cost of operations. Theory Centres are created wherever there are sufficient candidates for a regular Theory Centre. Candidates without access to a regular Theory Centre may apply for a Special Theory Centre to be established. All costs for Special Theory Centres must be met locally. Please refer to the Theory Syllabus for more information.

12 Second Associateship Diplomas

Candidates who have passed the Teacher's examination may obtain a Performer's Diploma by taking the entire Performer's ARCT examination. Candidates who have passed the Performer's examination will be exempt from the Performance of Pieces section of the Teacher's ARCT examination but must take all other sections, including the Teacher's written examination, to obtain the Teacher's ARCT Diploma. All of the required sections must be taken at the same session and completed within five years following successful completion of the Performer's practical examination. The ARCT Teacher's and Performer's examinations may not be attempted at the same session.

13 Adjustment of Marks

Marks are not adjusted to account for previously demonstrated abilities and skills. The examination marks reflect the examiner's opinion of the candidate's performance on the examination: they do not constitute the examiner's estimation of the candidate's innate musicality or potential for future development. Therefore, results of one examination do not prejudice the candidate's success on subsequent examinations in any way. The examiner's written evaluation of the examination is intended both to explain, in general terms, how the final grade was calculated and to assist the candidate in his or her musical development by pointing out musical strengths and weaknesses. There is no appeal of marks.

DETAILED MARKINGS TABLE

GUITAR EXAMINATIONS

Grades 1 to ARCT

Distinction 90-100
First Class Honours . . 80-89
Honours. 70-79

Grades 1 to 10

Pass 60-69

Grade 10/Teacher's ARCT

(Pass/Prerequisite) . . . (70)†

*Marks deducted for failure to memorize

**Memorization compulsory

†See "Supplemental Examinations" for marks less than (70)

CATEGORIES OF STUDY	GRADES 1-2	GRADES 3-6	GRADES 7-9	GRADE 10	ARCT TEACHER'S		ARCT PERFORMER'S
Performance of Pieces:							
LIST A	28	18	15	12			20
LIST B	28	18	15	12			20
LIST C		18	15	12 (42)	30	(21)	20 (70)
LIST D			15	12			20
LIST E				12			20
Memory	6	6	*	*	**		**
Technical Tests and Studies	28	20	20	20 (14)	10	(7)	
Ear Tests	10	10	10	10 (7)	10	(7)	
Sight Reading		10	10	10 (7)	10	(7)	
Viva Voce:							
a) Pedagogical Principles					20	(14)	
b) Applied Pedagogy					20	(14)	
Total Possible Marks	100	100	100	100(70)†	100	(70)†	100 (70)

14 Irregularities

Questions concerning irregularities in the conduct of an examination must be addressed to the Director of the Examination Department and postmarked within 48 hours of the examination. An irregularity is any violation of proper examination procedure as defined in the relevant Syllabus or other official Royal Conservatory of Music publications.

15 Supplemental Examinations

Supplemental Examinations are offered to eligible candidates for any section of a Grade 10 or Teacher's ARCT Practical examination in which a mark of 70 percent has not been achieved. To be eligible for a Supplemental examination, Grade 10 candidates must have achieved a minimum total mark of 60; Teacher's ARCT candidates must have achieved a minimum total mark of 65. Supplemental examinations are not available for the Performer's ARCT examination. In addition, candidates must have attempted a complete Grade 10 or ARCT examination before being eligible for a Supplemental examination. Supplemental examinations are offered during regularly scheduled examination sessions. Technical tests and studies must be re-tried together. All supplemental sections of a Grade 10 or ARCT examination must be taken at a single session, and must be completed within two years following the session of the initial practical examination. Candidates who do not complete the requirements within this period must re-apply for the entire examination.

PUBLISHERS AND COLLECTIONS

The following symbols, enclosed in parentheses, identify publishers and collections throughout the graded lists which follow. When no publisher or edition is indicated in these lists, the work is available in several standard editions. The editor's name occasionally appears following the indication of publisher, e.g., (SZ; Chiesa).

Symbol	Designation
AMA	*Antologia di musica antica* (SZ; Chiesa)
Assoc	Associated Music Publishers
Belw	Belwin Mills
Beran	Berandol
Berb/B	Berben
Bill	Billaudot
Boo	Boosey & Hawkes
Broek	Broekmans & Van Poppel
Cav	Caveat (E.C. Kerby)
CMC	Canadian Music Centre
Ches	J. & W. Chester
Co	Columbia Music Company
Cram	J.B. Cramer (London)
Dob	Doberman
EAG	Éditions aux Guitares (Basel)
EC	Elliott Chapin (Toronto)
EFM	Éditions françaises de musique
EGAL	*European Guitar and Lute Music* (Ric; Teuchert)
EGF	Éditions Gallant Frères

Symbol	Designation
EMB	Editio Musica Budapest
EMM	Ediciones Musicales Madrid
EMT	Éditions Musicales Transatlantiques
Esch	Max Eschig
EWH	Edition Wilhelm Hansen (Copenhagen)
Fab	Faber
FC	Franco Colombo
FH	Frederick Harris (Oakville)
GA	*Gitarren Archiv* (Schott)
H	Heugel
Hof	Hofmeister
Leeds	Leeds Music
Marks	E.B. Marks Music
Mills	Mills Music
MNS	Musical New Services (London)
Morn	Morning Music (Mississauga)
NM	Nova Music (Sussex)
Nov	Novello
Ox	Oxford
Peer	Peer
Per	Perrone Publications (Toronto)
Ric	Ricordi
Robb	Robbins Music (London)
Sal	Éditions Salabert
Scho	Schott
SchoF	Schott Frères (Brussels)
SZ	Suvini Zerboni
UME	Unión Musical Española
Uni	Universal Edition
VMG	*Virtuoso Music for Guitar* (Sherry-Brenner; Parkening)
Wat	Waterloo
Zan	Zanibon

GRADE ONE

REPERTOIRE

Candidates must be prepared to play TWO pieces by different composers from the following list. Compositions marked * are included in the *Royal Conservatory of Music Guitar Series: Grade 1 Repertoire and Studies Album* (Oakville: Frederick Harris, 1989). Each numbered item represents one selection for examination purposes.

LIST A

AGUADO, D.

1 *Moderato* (FH) *

ANONYMOUS

2 *Calleno costure me* (FH) *

BEAUVAIS, W.

3 *Dance 1* from *Guitar Pastels 1* (Cav)

BELL, S.

4 *Rêverie* from *Elementary Studies*, Bk. 4 (FH) *

CARULLI, F.

5 *Andante*, Op. 246 (FH) *
6 *Andante* (FH) *
7 *Andante grazioso*, Op. 211, No. 2 (FH) *
8 *Country Dance* (FH) *
9 *Waltz*, Op. 121, No. 1 (FH) *
10 *Anglaise*, Op. 121, No. 6 (FH) *
11 *Poco allegretto*, Op. 246 (FH) *
12 *Walzer*, Op. 241, No. 2 (FH) *
13 *Walzer* (FH) *

COGHLAN, M.

14 *Quasars* (FH) *
15 *Travellin'* (FH) *

DIABELLI, A.

16 *Andantino*, Op. 39, No. 2 (FH) *
17 *Vivace*, Op. 39, No. 3 (FH) *

DUKE, D.

18 *Sentimental Waltz* (FH) *

GAGNON, C.

19 *Chanson triste* from *La guitare enchantée* 1, No. 6 (Dob)
20 *Étude* from *La guitare enchantée* 1, No. 9 (Dob)
21 *Chanson vieilotte* from *La guitare enchantée* 1, No. 11 (Dob)
22 *Les Marionnettes* from *La guitare enchantée* 1, No. 24 (Dob)

GIULIANI, M.

23 *Écossaise*, Op. 33, No. 2 (FH) *
24 *Écossaise*, Op. 33, No. 3 (FH) *
25 *Écossaise*, Op. 33, No. 8 (FH) *
26 *Écossaise*, Op. 33, No. 10 (FH) *

KRAFT, N.

27 *Ancient Drums* (FH) *
28 *Ostinato* (FH) *

LE ROY, A.

29 *Bransle de Pictou* (FH) *

SANZ, G.

30 *Españoleta* from *Instrucción* (FH) *

SHEARER, A.

31 *Prelude* from *Classic Guitar Technique*, Vol. 1, No. 18 (FC; Shearer)

SOR, F.

32 *Allegro* from *Méthode* (FH) *
33 *Moderato*, Op. 35, No. 2 (FH) *

TANSMAN, A.

34 *Ostinato* from *Douze pièces faciles*, Vol. 1, No. 2 (Esch)
35 *Promenade* from *Douze pièces faciles*, Vol. 2, No. 1 (Esch)

TRADITIONAL

36 *A Bridge in London Time* (FH; McAllister) *
37 *Hockey Night in "O Canada"* (FH; McAllister) *
38 *The Ash Grove* from *La guitare enchantée* (FH; Gerrits) *
39 *Sakura* (EGF; Gallant) *
40 *Scarborough Fair* (FH; Kraft) *

STUDIES

Candidates must be prepared to play TWO studies of contrasting nature by different composers from the following list. Compositions marked * are included in the Studies section of the *Royal Conservatory of Music Guitar Series: Grade 1 Repertoire and Studies Album* (Oakville: Frederick Harris, 1989).

AGUADO, D.

41 *Moderato* [Study No. 1] from *Méthode* (FH) *
42 *Andante* [Study No. 4] (FH) *
43 *Moderato* [Study No. 5] (FH) *
44 *Allegretto* [Study No. 2] (FH) *
45 *Andante* [Study No. 7] (FH) *

BEAUVAIS, W.

46 *Via Brazil* [Study No. 14] (FH) *

BELL, S.

47 *High Mountains and Old Trees* [Study No. 12] from *Elementary Studies*, Bk. 5 (FH) *

CARCASSI, M.

48 *Étude 1* from *Classic Guitar*, Vol. 3, p. 9 (Leeds; Sealey & Trotter)

DIABELLI, A.

49 *Moderato*, Op. 39, No. 15 [Study No. 9] (FH) *

KRAFT, N.

50 *Grazioso* [Study No. 8] (FH) *

MCALLISTER, P.

51 *Jazzy Blues* [Study No. 15] (FH) *

SAGRERAS, J.

52 *Las primeras lecciones*, No. 46 (Ric)
53 *Las primeras lecciones*, No. 49 (Ric)
54 *Las primeras lecciones*, No. 60 (Ric)
55 *Las primeras lecciones*, No. 63 (Ric)
56 *Las primeras lecciones*, No. 64 (Ric)
57 *Las primeras lecciones*, No. 66 (Ric)

SHEARER, A.

58 *Prelude 12* from *Classic Guitar Technique*, Vol. 1, p. 47 (FC; Shearer)
59 *Étude 12* from *Classic Guitar Technique*, Vol. 1, p. 65 (FC; Shearer)

SOR, F.

60 *Allegretto* [Study No. 3] from *Méthode*, Op. 60, No. 8 (FH) *
61 *Andantino* [Study No. 6] from *Méthode* Op. 60 (FH) *

TÁRREGA, F.

62 *Study, TI ii-40* [Study No. 11] (FH) *

TRADITIONAL

63 *Ukrainian Folk Song* [Study No. 10] (FH) *

WILSON, D.

64 *Moderato* [Study No. 13] (FH) *

TECHNICAL REQUIREMENTS

In preparing for the technical portion of the examination, Candidates should consult the *Royal Conservatory of Music Guitar Series: Scales and Arpeggios Album* (Oakville: Frederick Harris, 1990).

SCALES M.M. ♩ = 92

The Candidate must be prepared to play the following scales in quarter notes in first position, ascending and descending. The scales must be fingered *i m*, rest stroke. Follow each scale with a V-I cadence in a four-note form. See Technical Requirements Examples, p. 51.

Major . . . . C—1 octave
G—2 octaves

Harmonic Minor . . . . . . A—1 octave
E—2 octaves

Melodic Minor . . . . A—1 octave
E—2 octaves

Chromatic . . . . starting on D—1 octave

EAR TESTS

13

A. RHYTHM

The Candidate will be required to sing, clap or tap the rhythm of a short melody after it has been played TWICE by the examiner.

Time Signature: 2/4 or 3/4

Rhythm Example

B. MELODY PLAYBACK

The Candidate will be required to play back a four-note melody based on the first three notes of the major scale which may contain repeated notes and/or a skip of a third after the examiner has:

1. named the key;

2. played the tonic triad ONCE; and

3. played the melody TWICE.

The melody may begin on any one of the three notes and may be in the key of C, F or G Major.

Melody Examples

GRADE TWO

REPERTOIRE

Candidates must be prepared to play TWO pieces, one from each of Lists A and B. Compositions marked * are included in the *Royal Conservatory of Music Guitar Series: Grade 2 Repertoire and Studies Album* (Oakville: Frederick Harris, 1989). Each numbered item represents one selection for examination purposes.

LIST A

CALVI, C.

1   *Pavaniglia* AND *Canario* (FH) *

FORD, T.

2   *There is a Lady* (FH) *

LE ROY, A.

3   *Paduane* (FH) *

ROSSETER, P.

4   *What is a Day?* (FH) *

SANZ, G.

5   *Españoleta* from *Instrucción* (FH) *
6   *Villanos* from *Instrucción* (FH) *

TRADITIONAL

7   *Greensleeves* (FH; Kraft) *

VISÉE, R. de

8   *Minuet* from *Suite in C Major* (FH) *
9   *Minuet in D Minor* from *Suite in E Minor* (FH) *

LIST B

AGUADO, D.

10   *Waltz* from *Méthode* (FH) *

CARCASSI, M.

11   *Sauteuse* (FH) *

CARULLI, F.

12   *Andante* (FH) *
13   *Andante*, Op. 211, No. 7 (FH) *
14   *Andantino in A Minor* (FH) *
15   *Walzer* (FH) *

DIABELLI, A.

16   *Allegretto*, Op. 39, No. 6 (FH) *

GAGNON, C.

17   *Adagio* from *La guitare enchantée*, No. 5 (Dob)

GIULIANI, M.

18   *Écossaise*, Op. 33, No. 1 (FH) *
19   *The Butterfly* from *Classic Guitar for Young People*, Vol. 3, p. 51 (Leeds; Sealey/Trottter)
20   *Écossaise*, Op. 33, No. 9 (FH) *
21   *Monferrina*, Op. 12, No. 1 (FH) *

JACKMAN, R.

22   *Chanson populaire* from *La guitare enchantée* (Dob) *

KATZ, B.

23   *School Blues* (FH) *

KRAFT, N.

24   *Barcarolle* (FH) *

LÉVEILLÉE, C.

25   *Soir d'hiver* from *Chansons et danses populaires* (Dob; Gagnon) *

MONTREUIL, G.

26   *Bahamas* from *Divertissements*, No. 2 (Dob)
27   *Calypso* from *Divertissements*, No. 7 (Dob)
28   *Carrousel* from *Divertissements*, No. 10 (Dob)
29   *Congo* from *Divertissements*, No. 11 (Dob)
30   *Romance* from *Divertissements*, No. 8 (Dob)
31   *Tango pour Mario* from *Divertissements*, No. 4 (Dob)

SAVIO, I.

32   *Lullaby* from *Ten Brazilian Folk Tunes* (Co) *

SCHUMANN, R.

33   *Stückchen* from *Album für die Jugend*, Op. 68, No. 5 (FH) *
34   *Trällerliedchen* from *Album für die Jugend*, Op. 68, No. 3 (FH) *

SOR, F.

35   *Allegretto*, Op. 44, No. 2 (FH) *
36   *Andante*, Op. 35, No. 1 (FH) *
37   *Andante*, Op. 44, No. 1 (FH) *
38   *Andantino*, Op. 60, No. 6 (FH) *
39   *Moderato*, Op. 31, No. 1 (FH) *

TANSMAN, A.

40   *12 pièces faciles*, Vol. 1, No. 1 (Esch)
41   *12 pièces faciles*, Vol. 1, No. 3 (Esch)
42   *12 pièces faciles*, Vol. 1, No. 5 (Esch)
43   *12 pièces faciles*, Vol. 2, No. 3 (Esch)
44   *12 pièces faciles*, Vol. 2, No. 4 (Esch)

TRADITIONAL

45 *V'là l'bon vent* (FH; Duke) *
46 *My Bark Canoe* (EGF; Gallant) *
47 *Twinkle, Twinkle, Little Star* from *Guitarrenmusik für Anfänger* (EMB; Vereczkey) *

STUDIES

Candidates must be prepared to play TWO studies of contrasting nature by different composers from the following list. Compositions marked * are included in the Studies section of the *Royal Conservatory of Music Guitar Series: Grade 2 Repertoire and Studies Album* (Oakville: Frederick Harris, 1989).

AGUADO, D.

48 *Study* [Study No. 1] (FH) *
49 *Study* [Study No. 1a] (FH) *
50 *Lección* [Study No. 5] from *Méthode* (FH) *
51 *Study* [Study No. 7] (FH) *
52 *Cantabile* [Study No. 10] (FH) *
53 *Animato* [Study No. 12] (FH) *
54 *Piacevole* [Study No. 14] (FH) *
55 *Study* [Study No. 16] (FH) *
56 *Study* [Study No. 18] (FH) *
57 *Study* [Study No. 20] (FH) *

BEAUVAIS, W.

58 *Dawn* [Study No. 22] from *Guitar Pastels 1* (EC) *
59 *Dance 1* [Study No. 23] from *Guitar Pastels 1* (EC) *

BENEDICT, R.

60 *20 Fantasy Études*, Vol. 1, No. 1 (Cav)
61 *20 Fantasy Études*, Vol. 1, No. 3 (Cav)

BROUWER, L.

62 *Études simples*, No. 2 (Esch)

CARCASSI, M.

63 *Study* [Study No. 17] (FH) *

CARULLI, F.

64 *Moderato* [Study No. 2] (FH) *
65 *Moderato* [Study No. 9] (FH) *

COGHLAN, M.

66 *The Blue Knight* [Study No. 26] (FH) *

DIABELLI, A.

67 *Scherzo*, Op. 39, No. 17 [Study No. 6] (FH) *
68 *Study*, Op. 39, No. 10 [Study No. 8] (FH) *

69 *Moderato*, Op. 39, No. 23 [Study No. 11] (FH) *
70 *Tempo di Minuetto*, Op. 39, No. 27 [Study No. 13] (FH) *

EVANS, R.

71 *Cascais* [Study No. 24] (FH) *

GALLANT, P.

72 *Study in Imitation* [Study No. 21] (EGF) *
73 *Study in Fifths* [Study No. 25] (EGF) *

GIULIANI, M.

74 *Leçon*, Op. 51, No. 1 [Study No. 3] (FH) *

SAGRERAS, J.

75 *Las primeras lecciones*, No. 53 (Ric)
76 *Las primeras lecciones*, No. 54 (Ric)
77 *Las primeras lecciones*, No. 55 (Ric)
78 *Las primeras lecciones*, No. 65 (Ric)
79 *Las primeras lecciones*, No. 75 (Ric)

SEALEY, R. and W. TROTTER

80 *Étude* from *Classic Guitar for Young People*, Vol. 3, No. 5, p. 18 (Leeds; Sealey & Trotter)

SOR, F.

81 *Andantino*, Op. 44, No. 9 [Study No. 15] (FH) *
82 *Andante*, Op. 44, No. 11 [Study No. 19] (FH) *

TÁRREGA, F.

83 *Study*, TI iii-32 [Study No. 4] (FH) *

WEINZWEIG, J.

84 *Rocking* [Study No. 27] (FH) *

TECHNICAL REQUIREMENTS

In preparing for the technical portion of the examination, Candidates should consult the *Royal Conservatory of Music Guitar Series: Scales and Arpeggios Album* (Oakville: Frederick Harris, 1990).

SCALES M.M. ♩ = 112

The Candidate must be prepared to play each of the following scales ascending and descending, in quarter notes in first position. Scales are to be fingered *i m*, rest stroke. Follow each scale with a V-I cadence in four-note forms. See Technical Requirements Examples, p. 51.

Major	D, B flat—1 octave
	F—2 octaves
Harmonic Minor	B, D—1 octave
	G—2 octaves
Melodic Minor	B, D—1 octave
	G—2 octaves
Chromatic	starting on A—1 octave

16

EAR TESTS

A.   RHYTHM

The Candidate will be required to sing, play or tap the rhythm of a short melody after the examiner has played it TWICE.

Time Signature: 2/4 or 3/4

Rhythm Examples

B.   INTERVALS

The Candidate will be required:

1. to sing or hum any of the following intervals after the first note has been played ONCE by the examiner;

OR (at the choice of the Candidate)

2. to identify any of the following intervals after each has been played ONCE in broken form by the examiner:

Major 3rd or Perfect 5th Above a given note.

C.   MELODY PLAYBACK

The Candidate will be required to play back a five-note melody based on the first five notes of a major scale which may contain one or more skips of a third after the examiner has:

1. named the key;

2. played the tonic triad ONCE; and

3. played the melody TWICE.

The melody may be in the key of C, F or G major and may begin on the tonic or dominant.

Melody Examples

GRADE THREE

REPERTOIRE

Candidates must be prepared to play THREE pieces, one from each of Lists A, B and C. The pieces must be by different composers. Compositions marked * are included in the *Royal Conservatory of Music Guitar Series: Grade 3 Repertoire and Studies Album* (Oakville: Frederick Harris, 1990). Each numbered item represents one selection for examination purposes.

LIST A

ANONYMOUS

1   Air (FH) *
2   Fortune My Foe from *Elizabethan Melodies*, Bk. 1, No. 7 in GA (Duarte/Rogers)
3   Sarabande from *La guitare enchantée*, Vol. 1, No. 17 (Dob)

BACH, J.S.

4   Minuet from *Suite for Keyboard*, BWV 822 (FH) *

BYRD, W.

5   Sellenger's Round from *Elizabethan Melodies*, Bk. 2, No. 5 in GA (Duarte/Rogers)

CALVI, C.

6   Allemanda (FH) *
7   Aria di Fiorenza (FH) *

DOWLAND, J.

8   Awake, Sweet Love from *Elizabethan Melodies*, Bk. 1, No. 5 in GA (Duarte/Rogers)

EDWARDS, R.

9   When Griping Griefs from *Elizabethan Melodies*, Bk. 2, No. 6 in GA (Duarte/Rogers)

HANDEL, G.F.

10   Prelude from *Sonata*, HWV 598 (FH) *

LE ROY, A.

11   Bransle haulbaroys (FH) *

NEUSIDLER, H.

12   Unser Köchin kan (FH) *

SANZ, G.

13   Paradetas AND Batalla from *Instrucción* (FH) *

TRADITIONAL

14   Danse de village from *Chansons* (Dob; Gagnon) *
15   Irish Jig from *Chansons* (Dob; Gagnon) *

VISÉE, R. de

16   Menuett (FH) *

LIST B

ANDES, M.

17   Canción (EAG)

CARCASSI, M.

18   Two Swiss Folk Songs from *Méthode* (FH) *
19   Marsch from *Méthode* (FH) *
20   Hunting Piece from *Méthode* (FH) *

CARULLI, F.

21   Andante, Op. 241 (FH) *
22   Andante from *Studi per chitarra*, No. 21 (SZ; Chiesa)
23   Andantino grazioso, Op. 241, No. 14 (FH) *
24   Carulli-Brevier, Vol. 2, No. 35 in GA
25   Carulli-Brevier, Vol. 2, No. 41 in GA
26   Carulli-Brevier, Vol. 2, No. 48 in GA
27   Larghetto from *Studi per chitarra*, No. 11 (SZ; Chiesa)
28   Walzer, Op. 124, No. 17 (FH) *
29   Walzer, Op. 241, No. 19 (FH) *

DIABELLI, A.

30   Menuett (FH) *

GIULIANI, M.

31   Andantino, Op. 50, No. 21 (FH) *
32   Larghetto, Op. 50, No. 17 (FH) *
33   Monferrina, Op. 12, No. 3 (FH) *
34   Monferrina, Op. 12, No. 6 (FH) *

MONTREUIL, G.

35   São Paolo from *Divertissements*, Vol. 2, No. 1 (Dob)
36   Pascale from *Divertissements*, Vol. 2, No. 3 (Dob)
37   Dolorès from *Divertissements*, Vol. 2, No. 4 (Dob)
38   Emmanuelle from *Divertissements*, Vol. 2, No. 5 (Dob)

PAGANINI, N.

39   Minuetto, M.S. 84, No. 26 (FH) *
40   Minuetto, M.S. 84, No. 27 (FH) *

ROSSINI, G.

41   Prelude (FH) *

SCHUMANN, R.

42   Soldatenmarsch, Op. 68, No. 2 (FH; Kraft) *
43   Melodie, Op. 68, No. 1 (FH; Kraft) *

SOR, F.

44   Andante, Op. 35, No. 14 (FH) *
45   Andantino, Op. 44, No. 3 (FH) *
46   Leçon, Op. 60, No. 5 (FH) *

TANSMAN, A.

47 *Intermezzo* from *12 pièces faciles*, Vol. 1, No. 10 (Esch)
48 *Serenade* from *12 pièces faciles*, Vol. 1, No. 11 (Esch)
49 *Petit chant* from *12 pièces faciles*, Vol. 2, No. 6 (Esch)
50 *Valsette* from *12 pièces faciles*, Vol. 2, No. 9 (Esch)
51 *Barcarolle* from *12 pièces faciles*, Vol. 2, No. 10 (Esch)

LIST C

BARNES, M.

52 *Song* (FH) *

COGHLAN, M.

53 *Blues* (FH) *
54 *The Blue Calliope* (FH) *

GAGNON, C.

55 *The Frog Blues* (FH) *

KRAFT, N.

56 *Reminiscence* (FH) *

SAVIO, I.

57 *Maracatu* from *Ten Brazilian Folk Tunes* (Co)
58 *Modinha* from *Ten Brazilian Folk Tunes* (Co)
59 *Lullaby* AND *Sapo Jururu* from *Ten Brazilian Folk Tunes* (Co)
60 *Samba-Lelê* from *Ten Brazilian Folk Tunes* (Co) *

WILSON, D.

61 *Carulli Variations* (FH) *

STUDIES

Candidates must be prepared to play TWO studies of contrasting nature by different composers from the following list. Compositions marked * are included in the Studies section of the *Royal Conservatory of Music Guitar Series: Grade 3 Repertoire and Studies Album* (Oakville: Frederick Harris, 1990).

AGUADO, D.

62 *Andante mosso* [Study No. 1] from *Méthode* (FH) *
63 *Allegretto* [Study No. 2] from *Méthode* (FH) *
64 *Allegretto* [Study No. 3] from *Méthode* (FH) *
65 *Allegretto* [Study No. 4] from *Méthode* (FH) *
66 *Andante* [Study No. 5] from *Méthode* (FH) *
67 *[Moderato]* [Study No. 6] from *Méthode* (FH) *

BEAUVAIS, W.

68 *Mirror dance* [Study No. 11] from *Primary Colours* (FH) *

BENEDICT, R.

69 *Twenty Fantasy Études*, Vol. 1, No. 2 (Cav)
70 *Twenty Fantasy Études*, Vol. 1, No. 4 (Cav)
71 *Twenty Fantasy Études*, Vol. 1, No. 5 (Cav)

BROUWER, L.

72 *Études simples*, No. 1 (Esch)
73 *Études simples*, No. 4 (Esch)

CARULLI, F.

74 *Study* [Study No. 7] (FH) *
75 *Allegretto*, Op. 114 [Study No. 8] (FH) *

GALLANT, P.

76 *Lullaby* [Study No. 12] (FH) *

SAGRERAS, J.

77 *Las primeras lecciones*, No. 67 (BA)
78 *Las primeras lecciones*, No. 72 (BA)
79 *Las primeras lecciones*, No. 80 (BA)
80 *Las primeras lecciones*, No. 82 (BA)
81 *Las primeras lecciones*, No. 83 (BA)
82 *Las primeras lecciones*, No. 84 (BA)
83 *Las primeras lecciones*, No. 85 (BA)

SOR, F.

84 *[Exercise for Sixths]*, No. 4 from *Méthode* [Study No. 9] (FH) *
85 *Allegretto*, Op. 60, No. 7 [Study No. 10] (FH) *

TRADITIONAL

86 *This Old Man, Man* [Study No. 13] (EGF; Gallant) *

TECHNICAL REQUIREMENTS

In preparing for the technical portion of the examination, Candidates should consult the *Royal Conservatory of Music Guitar Series: Scales and Arpeggios Album* (Oakville: Frederick Harris, 1990).

SCALES M.M. ♩ = 120

Scales are to be played ascending and descending, in quarter notes in first position. Scales are to be fingered *i m, m a*, rest stroke. Follow each scale with a V-I cadence in four-note forms. See Technical Requirements Examples, p. 51.

Major	E flat—1 octave
	A, E—2 octaves
Harmonic Minor	C, C sharp—1 octave
	F sharp—2 octaves
Melodic Minor	C, C sharp—1 octave
	F sharp—2 octaves
Chromatic	starting on E—1 octave

EAR TESTS

A. RHYTHM

The Candidate will be required to sing, play or tap the rhythm of a short melody after the examiner has played it TWICE.

Time Signature: 2/4 or 3/4

Rhythm Examples

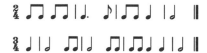

B. INTERVALS

The Candidate will be required:

1. to sing or hum any of the following intervals after the first note has been played ONCE by the examiner;

OR (at the discretion of the Candidate)

2. to identify any of the following intervals after each has been played ONCE in broken form by the examiner:

Major 3rd , Perfect 5th or Octave Above a given note and Minor 3rd or Perfect 5th Below a given note.

C. MELODY PLAYBACK

The Candidate will be required to play back a five-note melody based on the first five notes of a major scale which may contain a skip of a third and/or fifth after the examiner has:

1. named the key;

2. played the tonic triad ONCE; and

3. played the melody TWICE.

The melody may be in the key of C, F, G or D major and may begin on the tonic or mediant.

Melody Examples

SIGHT READING

The candidate will be required:

A. to play a simple short passage in 4/4 time in the key of D or G major; AND

B. to clap or tap a rhythmic pattern in 3/4 time with half, quarter and eighth notes. In order to achieve full marks, the student must maintain a steady pace and metrical accentuation. The sight reading example indicates the approximate degree of difficulty.

Sight Reading Example

GRADE FOUR

REPERTOIRE

Candidates must be prepared to play THREE pieces, one from each of Lists A, B and C. The pieces must be by different composers. Compositions marked * are included in the *Royal Conservatory of Music Guitar Series: Grade 4 Repertoire and Studies Album* (Oakville: Harris, 1990). Each numbered item represents one selection for examination purposes.

LIST A

ANONYMOUS

1   *13 Pieces from the Fitzwilliam Virginal Book*, No. 180 (Nov; Duarte)
2   *13 Pieces from the Fitzwilliam Virginal Book*, No. 188 (Nov; Duarte)
3   *Allemande* (FH) *
4   *Balletto* (FH) *

DOWLAND, J.

5   *My Lord Willoughby's Welcome Home*, Poulton No. 66 (FH) *
6   *Mrs. Winter's Jump*, Poulton No. 55 (FH) *

FORD, T.

7   *Since First I Saw Your Face* from *Elizabethan Melodies*, Bk. 2 in GA

LE ROY, A.

8   *Almande "La Mon Amy La"* from *Premier livre* (FH) *

LOGY, J.A.

9   *Aria* AND *Sarabande* from *Suite IX* (FH) *

NEUSIDLER, M.

10   *Der Fuggerin Tanz* from *Teütsch Lautenbuch* (FH) *

PHALÈSE, P.

11   *Almande Loreyne* from EGAL, Vol. 6
12   *Passemese* from EGAL, Vol. 6

RONCALLI, L.

13   *Sarabanda* from *Capricci armonici* (FH) *
14   *Gavotta I* from *Capricci armonici* (FH) *
15   *Gavotta II* from *Capricci armonici* (FH) *

SANZ, G.

16   Any TWO of *Matachin, Rujero, Zarabanda* from *Instrucción* (FH) *
17   *Españoleta* from *Instrucción* in EGAL, Vol. 5

TRADITIONAL

18   *Le roi Dagobert* from *Chansons et danses populaires* (Dob; Gagnon) *

VISÉE, R. de

19   *Sarabande* from *Suite XI, Livre de pièces* (FH) *

LIST B

ANDES, M.

20   *Vals* (EAG)

BENEDICT, R.

21   *Divertimenti*, No. 5 (Wat)

CARCASSI, M.

22   *Larghetto* from *Carcassi-Brevier*, Vol. 3, No. 41 in GA
23   *Waltz* from *Carcassi-Brevier*, Vol. 3, No. 49 in GA

CARULLI, F.

24   *Allegretto*, Op. 241 (FH) *
25   *Andante*, Op. 241 (FH) *
26   *Rondo*, Op. 241 (FH) *
27   *Carulli-Brevier*, Vol. 2, No. 45 in GA
28   *Carulli-Brevier*, Vol. 2, No. 46 in GA
29   *Carulli-Brevier*, Vol. 2, No. 50 in GA

CHOPIN, F.

30   *Prélude* from *24 Präludien für das Pianoforte*, Op. 28, No. 7 (FH; Kraft) *

GIULIANI, M.

31   *Divertimento*, Op. 40, No. 11 (FH) *

MOZART, W.A.

32   *Minuet*, K.2/58 (FH) *

PAGANINI, N.

33   *Minuetto*, M.S. 43 (FH) *
34   *Kleine Stücke* (Scho; Vereczkey), Nos. 3 AND 17

SCHUMANN, R.

35   *Erster Verlust* from *Album für die Jugend*, Op. 68, No.16 (FH; Kraft) *

SOR, F.

36   *Leon* from *24 leçons progressives*, Op. 31, No. 4 (FH) *
37   *Waltz*, Op. 8, No. 2 (FH) *
38   *Waltz*, Op. 2, No. 2 (FH) *

LIST C

DUKE, D.

39 *Game of Fourths* (FH) *

GAGNON, C.

40 *Cornemuse* from *La guitare enchantée* 1, No. 18 (Dob)

KATZ, B.

41 *Gentle Waltz* from *The Amethyst Collection* (FH) *

LECLERCQ, N.

42 *Cyclamen* from *Six couleurs* (SchoF) *

NØRHOLM, I.

43 *Interlude* from *Sonata for Guitar*, Op. 69 (EWH) *

RIERA, R.

44 *Nostalgia* from *Four Venezuelan Pieces* (Uni)

SUGÁR, R.

45 *Gyermekdalok* from *Ungarische Kinderlieder* (EMB; Adrovicz) *

TANSMAN, A.

46 *Tarantella* from *12 pièces faciles*, Vol. 1, No. 7 (Esch)
47 *Toccata* from *12 pièces faciles*, Vol. 1, No. 9 (Esch)
48 *A l'espagnole* from *12 pièces faciles*, Vol. 2, No. 11 (Esch)

TÁRREGA, F.

49 *Lágrima* (Prelude, TI i-17) (FH) *

STUDIES

Candidates must be prepared to play TWO studies of contrasting nature by different composers from the following list. Compositions marked * are included in the Studies section of the *Royal Conservatory of Music Guitar Series: Grade 4 Repertoire and Studies Album* (Oakville: Frederick Harris, 1990).

AGUADO, D.

50 *Grazioso* [Study No. 1] from *Méthode* (FH) *
51 *Andantino* [Study No. 2] from *Méthode* (FH) *
52 *Allegretto* [Study No. 3] from *Méthode* (FH) *
53 *Andante* [Study No. 4] from *Méthode* (FH) *
54 *Leçon* [Study No. 5] from *Méthode* (FH) *
55 [*Moderato*] [Study No. 6] from *Méthode* (FH) *

BROUWER, L.

56 *Études simples*, No. 5 (Esch)
57 *Études simples*, No. 8 (Esch)

CARULLI, F.

58 *Andantino* [Study No. 10] (FH) *

DIABELLI, A.

59 *Trenta studi facili*, Op. 39, No. 30 (SZ; Company)

GIULIANI, M.

60 *Studi per chitarra*, No. 43 (SZ; Chiesa)
61 *Allegretto* [Study No. 7], Op. 50, No. 22 (FH) *

KRAFT, N.

62 *Scherzino* [Study No. 11] (FH) *
63 *Study in Seven* [Study No. 13] (FH) *

SOR, F.

64 *Studi per chitarra*, No. 37 (SZ; Chiesa)
65 *Andante allegro* [Study No. 8], Op. 6, No. 2 (FH) *
66 *Allegro moderato* [Study No. 9], Op. 6, No. 1 (FH) *

TÁRREGA, F.

67 *Study* [Study No. 12], TI ii-26 (FH) *

WILSON, D.

68 *Moderato* [Study No. 14] (FH) *

TECHNICAL REQUIREMENTS

In preparing for the technical portion of the examination, Candidates should consult the *Royal Conservatory of Music Guitar Series: Scales and Arpeggios Album* (Oakville: Frederick Harris, 1990).

SCALES M.M. ♩ = 52

The Candidate must be prepared to play the following scales in triplet eighth notes in first position, ascending and descending. The scales must be fingered *i m* and *m a* and played with free strokes and rest strokes. Follow each scale with a V-I cadence in four-note forms. See Technical Requirements Examples, p. 51.

Major	B, D flat—1 octave
	A flat, F sharp—2 octaves
Harmonic Minor	D sharp, B flat—1 octave
	F, G sharp—2 octaves
Melodic Minor	D sharp, B flat—1 octave
	F, G sharp—2 octaves
Chromatic	starting on A—2 octaves

SLUR SCALES M.M. ♩ = 52

Slur scales must be played ascending and descending in eighth notes, in first position, single slurs.

Major	D, A—1 octave

EAR TESTS

A. RHYTHM

The Candidate will be required to sing, play or tap the rhythm of a short melody after the examiner has played it TWICE.

Time Signature: 2/4 or 6/8

Rhythm Examples

B. INTERVALS

The Candidate will be required:

1. to sing or hum any of the following intervals after the first note has been played ONCE by the examiner;

OR (at the choice of the Candidate)

2. to identify any of the following intervals after each has been played ONCE in broken form by the examiner:

Major and Minor 3rd, Perfect 4th, 5th and octave Above a given note; Minor 3rd, Perfect 5th and octave Below a given note.

C. MELODY PLAYBACK

The Candidate will be required to play back a melody of about six notes based on the first five notes of a major scale after the examiner has:

1. named the key;

2. played the tonic triad ONCE; and

3. played the melody TWICE.

The melody may begin on the tonic, mediant or dominant of C, F, G or D major.

Melody Example

SIGHT READING

The Candidate will be required:

A. to play a short simple melody, in 4/4 time, in the key of D, F, G or A major; AND

B. to clap or tap the rhythm of a melody in 3/4 or 4/4 time. In order to achieve full marks, the Candidate must maintain a steady pace and metrical accentuation. The sight reading example indicates the approximate degree of difficulty.

Sight Reading Example

GRADE FIVE

REPERTOIRE

Candidates must be prepared to play THREE pieces, one from each of Lists A, B, and C. Compositions marked * are included in the *Royal Conservatory of Music Guitar Series: Grade 5 Repertoire and Studies Album* (Oakville: Frederick Harris, 1990). Each numbered item represents one selection for examination purposes.

LIST A

ANONYMOUS

1   Kemp's Jig (FH) *
2   Any TWO of Nos. 1, 3, 4, 5 from *Six Lute Pieces of the Renaissance* (Co; Chilesotti)
3   *13 Pieces from the Fitzwilliam Virginal Book*, No. 161 (Nov; Duarte)
4   *Danza* AND *Corrente* from EGAL, Vol. 1, pp. 7, 11
5   *Gaillard* from EGAL, Vol. 3, p. 11 (Ric; Teuchert)

BARON, E.G.

6   *Gigue* from *Music for Solo Guitar*, Vol. 1, No. 7 (Dob)

CAMPION, T.

7   *Gigue* from *Classical Montage* (Wat; Mills)

CUTTING, F.

8   *Greensleeves* from *International Anthology*, p. 87 (FC; Bellow)

DOWLAND, J.

9   *Almain*, Poulton No. 49 (FH) *
10   *Lady Laiton's Almain*, Poulton No. 48 (FH) *

GAULTIER, D.

11   *Tombeau* from EGAL, Vol. 4

HOFFER, J.J.

12   *Gigue* from *Music for Solo Guitar*, Vol. 1, No. 9 (Dob)

HOVE, J. van den

13   *Toccata* from *Music for Solo Guitar*, Vol. 1, No. 4 (Dob)

JOHNSON, R.

14   *Alman*, Sundermann No. 7 (FH) *

LOGY, J.A.

15   Any TWO of *Capriccio*, *Gavotte*, *Gigue* from *Partita in A Minor* (Uni; Scheit)

MUDARRA, A.

16   *Gallarda* from *Tres libros*, Vol. 1 (FH) *

NEUSIDLER, H.

17   *Wayss mir ein hubsche Mulnerin* AND *Hupff auff* from *Arie e danze*, Vol. 2, pp. 1-2 (Ric; Tonazzi)
18   *Der Ziegler in der Hechken* from *Arie e danze*, Vol. 2, p. 3 (Ric; Tonazzi)

PURCELL, H.

19   *Hornpipe* from *Four Pieces* (Fab; Bream)
20   *A New Irish Tune* from *Classical Montage* (Wat; Mills)

ROBINSON, T.

21   *Walking in a Country Towne* from *Five Pieces* (Uni; Scheit)
22   *Toy* from *Toy, Air and Gigue* (Uni; Scheit)
23   *Gigue* from *Toy, Air and Gigue* (Uni; Scheit)

SANZ, G.

24   *Villanos* from *Instrucción*, Vol. 2 (Wat; Mills) *
25   *Españoleta* from *Instrucción*, Vol. 2 (FH) *

VISÉE, R. de

26   *Sarabande* from EGAL, Vol. 4, p. 14
27   *Prelude* from *Suite in D Minor, Livre de guittarre* (FH) *

WEISS, S.L.

28   *Menuet* from *Suite XV in F Major* (FH) *

LIST B

AMBROSIUS, H.

29   *Impressionen: Traum* (B; Gilardino)

ANONYMOUS

30   *Spanish Romance* from *Jeux interdits: musique du film* (EMT; Yepes)

BARRIOS MANGORÉ, A.

31   *Minuet en do* from *Guitar Works*, p. 5 (Belw; Stover)

BENEDICT, R.

32   *Divertimenti*, No. 2 (Wat)

CARCASSI, M.

33   *Andantino grazioso* from *Carcassi-Brevier*, Vol. 2, No. 29 in GA

CARULLI, F.

34   *Rondo*, Op. 241 (FH) *

CASTELNUOVO-TEDESCO, M.

35   *Tempo di siciliana* from *Appunti*, Vol. 1, No. 1 (SZ)

FERRER, J.

36   *El amable* (FH) *

GERRITS, P.

37   *Prelude* from *Music for Solo Guitar*, Vol. 1, p. 27 (Dob)

GIULIANI, M.

38   *Allegretto*, Op. 51, No. 15 (FH) *
39   *Allegro*, Op. 40, No. 6 (FH) *
40   *Andante espressivo*, Op. 40, No. 7 (FH) *
41   *Grazioso*, Op. 50, No. 23 (FH) *
42   *Divertimenti*, Op. 37, No. 6 in GA
43   *Divertimenti*, Op. 37, No. 8 in GA
44   *Divertimenti*, Op. 37, No. 11 in GA
45   *Divertimenti*, Op. 37, No. 12 in GA

24

MOLINO, F.

46   *Six Rondos*, No. 4 in GA
47   *Six Rondos*, No. 5 in GA

MOZART, W.A.

48   *Allegro*, K. 3 (FH; Kraft) *

PAGANINI, N.

49   *Sonatina* from *Kleine Stücke*, No. 7 (Scho; Vereczkey)

SOR, F.

50   *Allegretto*, Op. 35, No. 8 (FH) *
51   *Studi per chitarra*, No. 45 (SZ; Chiesa)
52   *Studi per chitarra*, No. 48 (SZ; Chiesa)
53   *Waltz* from *Second Set of Divertimenti*, Op. 2, No. 5 (Ox; Quine)

TÁRREGA, F.

54   *Adelita* (FH) *

LIST C

BEAUVAIS, W.

55   *Lullabye-bye* (FH) *
56   *Children's Song* (FH) *

CAMILLERI, C.

57   *Shadow of the Moons* from *Four African Sketches* (FH) *

COGHLAN, M.

58   *Prelude* AND *Blues* (FH) *
59   *Tango* (FH) *

DISERA, P.

60   *Waltz* (FH) *

FEGGELEN, C. van

61   *Homage to Luiz Bonfa* (FH) *

GALLANT, P.

62   *Lacrymosa* (FH) *

JAMIESON, D.

63   *Shadows* AND *La belle jarretière verte* (FH) *

RIERA, R.

64   *Melancolia* from *Four Venezuelan Pieces* (Uni)

STUDIES

Candidates must be prepared to play TWO studies of contrasting nature by different composers from the following list. Compositions marked * are included in the Studies section of the *Royal Conservatory of Music Guitar Series: Grade 5 Repertoire and Studies Album* (Oakville: Frederick Harris, 1990).

AGUADO, D.

65   *Andantino* [Study No. 1] from *Méthode* (FH) *
66   *Allegretto* [Study No. 2] from *Méthode* (FH) *
67   *Allegretto* [Study No. 3] from *Méthode* (FH) *

BELLAVANCE, G.

68   *Étude I* from *Music for Solo Guitar*, Vol. 2, No. 9 (Dob)
69   *Étude II* from *Music for Solo Guitar*, Vol. 2, No. 10 (Dob)

BENEDICT, R.

70   *Twenty Fantasy Études*, Vol. 1, No. 11 (Cav)
71   *Fughettas*, No. 1 (Wat)

BROUWER, L.

72   *Études simples*, No. 3 (Esch)

COSTE, N.

73   *Allegretto* [Study No. 5] (FH) *

CARCASSI, M.

74   *Moderato* [Study No. 6], Op. 60, No. 2 (FH) *
75   *Allegro* [Study No. 4], Op. 60, No. 9 (FH) *
76   *Allegretto* [Study No. 7], Op. 60, No. 10 (FH) *

EVANS, R.

77   *Samba latino* [Study No. 17] (FH) *

FEGGELEN, C. van

78   *So Unusual (Study III)* [Study No. 16] (FH) *

GALLANT, P.

79   *Study in Alternating Notes* [Study No. 14] (FH) *

GIULIANI, M.

80   *Vivace* [Study No. 9], Op. 48, No. 1 (FH) *

JOACHIM, O.

81   *Energico* [Study No. 12] from *6 Stücke* AND *Mässig schnell* [Study No. 13] from *6 Stücke* (FH) *

KATZ, B.

82   *Study* [Study No. 15] (FH) *

SAGRERAS, J.

83   *Las terceras lecciones*, No. 32 (Ric)
84   *Las terceras lecciones*, No. 36 (Ric)
85   *Las terceras lecciones*, No. 38 (Ric)
86   *Las cuartas lecciones*, No. 10 (Ric)
87   *Las cuartas lecciones*, No. 12 (Ric)
88   *Las cuartas lecciones*, No. 15 (Ric)
89   *Las quintas lecciones*, No. 9 (Ric)

SOR, F.

90 *Allegretto* [Study No. 8], Op. 35, No. 22 (FH) *
91 *Moderato* [Study No. 10], Op. 35, No. 17 (FH) *
92 *Andante* [Study No. 11], Op. 35, No. 13 (FH) *

TANSMAN, A.

93 *Triolets* from *12 pièces faciles*, Vol. 1, No. 12 (Esch)
94 *Étude* from *12 pièces faciles*, Vol. 2, No. 12 (Esch)

TECHNICAL REQUIREMENTS

In preparing for the technical portion of the examination, Candidates should consult the *Royal Conservatory of Music Guitar Series: Scales and Arpeggios Album* (Oakville: Frederick Harris, 1990).

SCALES M.M. ♩ = 58

The Candidate must be prepared to play the following scales in triplet eighth notes and sixteenth notes, ascending and descending. The scales should be fingered *i m, m a* and *i a*, and played with free strokes and rest strokes. **Scales are NOT to be fingered as first position, open-string scales.** Follow each scale with a I-IV-V-I cadence in a four-note form. See Technical Requirements Examples, p. 51.

Major . . . . C, G, D, A, E flat, A flat, D flat—2 octaves

Harmonic Minor . . . . . . A, E, B, F sharp, C, F, B flat—2 octaves

Melodic Minor . . . . A, E, B, F sharp, C, F, B flat—2 octaves

Chromatic . . . . starting on E—2 octaves

SLUR SCALES M.M. ♩ = 66

Major . . . . C, G—1 octave

REPEATED NOTE SCALES M.M. ♩ = 66

Ascending and descending in sixteenth notes to be fingered *i m*, rest stroke.

Major . . . . C, G, D, A, E flat, A flat, D flat—2 octaves

Harmonic Minor . . . . . . A, E, B, F sharp, C, F, B flat—2 octaves

Melodic Minor . . . . A, E, B, F sharp, C, F, B flat—2 octaves

EAR TESTS

A. RHYTHM

The Candidate will be required to sing, play or tap the rhythm of a short melody after the examiner has played it TWICE.

Time Signature: 3/4 or 6/8

Rhythm Examples

B. INTERVALS   25

The Candidate will be required:

1. to sing or hum any of the following intervals after the first note has been played ONCE by the examiner;

OR (at the choice of the Candidate)

2. to identify any of the following intervals after each has been played ONCE in broken form by the examiner.

Major and Minor 3rds, Major and Minor 6ths, Perfect 4ths, 5ths and octaves Above a given note; Major and Minor 3rds and Perfect 5ths and octaves Below a given note.

C. MELODY PLAYBACK

The Candidate will be required to play back a melody of approximately seven notes, based on the first five notes and the upper tonic of a major scale after the examiner has:

1. named the key;

2. played the tonic triad ONCE; and

3. played the melody TWICE.

The melody may begin on the tonic, mediant or dominant of the key of C, F, G or D major.

Melody Example

SIGHT READING

The Candidate will be required:

A. to play a short passage in a major or minor key equal in difficulty to a Grade 3 piece; AND

B. to clap or tap the rhythm of a melody in 3/4 or 4/4 time. In order to achieve full marks, the Candidate must maintain a steady pace and metrical accentuation. The sight reading example indicates the approximate degree of difficulty.

Sight Reading Example

THEORY CO-REQUISITE

Preliminary Rudiments OR

Grade 1 Rudiments OR

Grade 2 Rudiments

GRADE SIX

REPERTOIRE

Candidates must be prepared to play THREE pieces, one from each of Lists A, B and C. Compositions marked * are included in the *Royal Conservatory of Music Guitar Series: Grade 6 Repertoire and Studies Album* (Oakville: Frederick Harris, 1990). Each numbered item represents one selection for examination purposes.

LIST A

ANONYMOUS

1   *Six Lute Pieces of the Renaissance*, Nos. 2 AND 6 (Co; Chilesotti)

BACH, J.S.

2   *Bourrée* from *Lute Suite No. 1 in E Minor*, BWV 996 (FH) *
3   *Sarabande* from *Violoncello Suite No. 3*, BWV 1007 in GA
4   *Sarabande* from *Violin Partita*, BWV 1002 (FH; Kraft) *

CABEZÓN, A.

5   *Himno a tres* from *Tre composizioni* (SZ; Hinojosa)

DOWLAND, J.

6   *Air* from *Air and Galliard* (Uni; Scheit)
7   *Galliard*, Poulton No. 42, parts A, C, E (FH) *

FARNABY, G.

8   *Tower Hill* from *Five Pieces* in GA

FUHRMANN, G.L.

9   *Lied* AND *Ballett* from *EGAL*, Vol. 2, p. 9

HANDEL, G.F.

10   *Gavotte* from *Classical Montage* (Wat; Mills)

HOFFER, K.

11   *Gigue* from *Music for Solo Guitar*, Vol. 1, p. 16 (Dob)

MILAN, L.

12   *Pavane* from *El maestro* in *EGAL*, Vol. 5, p. 12
13   *Pavane III* from *El maestro* (FH) *

PACHELBEL, J.

14   *Paysanne* from *EGAL*, Vol. 2, p. 12

PHALÈSE, P.

15   *Galliarde* from *EGAL*, Vol. 6, p. 5

POLAK, J.

16   *Galliarde* from *EGAL*, Vol. 7, p. 14

PURCELL, H.

17   *Air* AND *Minuet* from *Four Pieces* (Fab; Bream)

REUSNER, E.

18   *Sonatina* from *EGAL*, Vol. 2, pp. 10-11

SANZ, G.

19   *Pavanas* from *Instrucción* (FH) *
20   *Rujero* from *Spanish Suite* (Wat; Mills) *
21   *La Caballeria de Napoles* from *Spanish Suite* (Wat; Mills)

STÖLZEL, G.H.

22   *Bourrée* from *Music for Solo Guitar*, Vol. 1, p. 15 (Dob)

VISÉE, R. de

23   *Passacaille* from *Suite in re minore* (Ric; Paolini)
24   *Bourrée* AND *Two Minuets* from *Suite in re minore* (Ric; Paolini)

WEISS, S.L.

25   *Courente* (FH) *
26   *Eleven Pieces*, No. 2 (Ric; Skiera)
27   *Eleven Pieces*, No. 3 (Ric; Skiera)
28   *Eleven Pieces*, No. 6 (Ric; Skiera)
29   *Prelude* from *Lute Suite No. 4* (FH) *

LIST B

AMBROSIUS, H.

30   Any TWO of *Neckerei, Melancholie, Exotischer Tanz* from *Impressionen* (Berb; Gilardino)

BARRIOS MANGORÉ, A.

31   *Mabelita* from *Guitar Works*, p. 13 (Belw; Stover)
32   *Madrecita* from *Guitar Works*, p. 17 (Belw; Stover)

CARULLI, F.

33   *Larghetto*, Op. 124, No. 23 (FH) *

CASTELNUOVO-TEDESCO, M.

34   *Appunti*, Vol. 1, No. 2 (SZ)

COSTE, N.

35   *Andantino* from *Guitar Works*, Vol. 9 (Chanterelle; Wynberg)
36   *Pastorale* from *Guitar Works*, Vol. 9 (Chanterelle; Wynberg)
37   *Valse* (FH) *
38   *Valse in A Major* from *Guitar Works*, Vol. 9 (Chanterelle; Wynberg)

FERRER, J.

39 *Vals* (FH) *

GIULIANI, M.

40 *Divertimento*, Op. 37, No. 3 (FH) *
41 *Divertimento*, Op. 37, No. 5 (FH) *
42 *Divertimento*, Op. 40, No. 12 (FH) *

GLUCK, C.W.

43 *Ballet* from *Album of Guitar Solos* (Co; Segovia)

KELLY, B.

44 *Aubade* from *Aubade, Toccata and Nocturne*, No. 1 (Nov)

MORENO-TORROBA, F.

45 *Preambulo* from *Pièces caractéristiques*, Vol. 1 in GA

PERRONE, J.

46 *Vals* (Per)

PONCE, M.

47 *Tres canciones populares mexicanas*, No. 1 in GA
48 Any TWO of Nos. 5, 6, 10, 11 from *Preludes*, Vols. 1 and 2 in GA

SATIE, E.

49 *Gymnopédie No. 1* in VMG

SOR, F.

50 *Minuet*, Op. 22 (FH) *
51 *Minuet*, Op. 25 (FH) *

TANSMAN, A.

52 *Prélude* from *Hommage à Chopin* (Esch)
53 *Suite in modo polonico*, No. 1 (Esch)
54 *Suite in modo polonico*, No. 2 (Esch)
55 *Suite in modo polonico*, No. 3 (Esch)
56 *Suite in modo polonico*, No. 4 (Esch)
57 *Suite in modo polonico*, No. 5 (Esch)
58 *Suite in modo polonico*, No. 6 (Esch)
59 *Suite in modo polonico*, No. 8 (Esch)

TÁRREGA, F.

60 *Pavana* (FH) *

VILLA-LOBOS, H.

61 *Prelude* No. 4 (Esch)

LIST C

27

BALADA, L.

62 *Lento* from *Suite No. 1* (Co; Lima) *

BEAUVAIS, W.

63 *Walking Song* (FH)

BENEDICT, R.

64 *Divertimenti*, No. 1 (Wat)
65 *Fughettas*, No. 2, p. 84 (Wat)

CAMILLERI, C.

66 *Folk Prelude* from *Four African Sketches* (Cram) *

CHIEREGHIN, S.

67 *Pour Bérénice* from *Trois chansons jouées* (FH) *
68 *Canzone* (FH)

DUKE, D.

69 *Arioso cantabile* (FH) *

FEGGELEN, C. van

70 *Peruvian Waltz* (FH) *

FEUERSTEIN, R.

71 *Dance* from *Three Pieces for Guitar* (Morn) *

FREEDMAN, H.

72 *Sicilienne* (FH; Feuerstein) *

GAGNON, C.

73 *Rêverie* from *Music for Solo Guitar*, Vol. 1, p. 29 (Dob)

GERRITS, P.

74 *Reflets* from *Music For Solo Guitar*, Vol. 3, No. 17 (Dob)

LAURO, A.

75 *Registro* from *Suite Venezolana* (Broek; Diaz) *

LE BLOND, L.

76 *Esquisse* from *Music For Solo Guitar*, Vol. 1, No. 19 (Dob)

PENNYCOOK, B.

77 *Quasi-Marcia* from *August Suite* (FH) *

REPOULIS, M.

78 *Reflections of Dali* AND *View of Toledo* (NM)

28

WALTON, W.

79   *Bagatelle No. 2* from *Five Bagatelles* (Ox; Bream) *

WEINZWEIG, J.

80   *Contrasts*, No. 1 (FH)

STUDIES

Candidates must be prepared to play TWO studies of contrasting nature by different composers from the following list. Compositions marked * are included in the Studies section of the *Royal Conservatory of Music Guitar Series: Grade 6 Repertoire and Studies Album* (Oakville: Frederick Harris, 1990).

AGUADO, D.

81   *Estudio 5* [Study No. 2] from *Méthode complète* (FH)*

BEAUVAIS, W.

82   *Perpetuum Mobile* [Study No. 12] from *Guitar Pastels I* (FH)*

BENEDICT, R.

83   *Twenty Fantasy Études*, Vol. 2, No. 12 (Cav)
84   *Twenty Fantasy Études*, Vol. 2, No. 17 (Cav)

BROUWER, L.

85   *Études simples*, No. 6 (Esch)
86   *Études simples*, No. 7 (Esch)

BRÜHL, K.W.

87   *Deux études* (No. 1 only) from *Music for Solo Guitar*, Vol. 3, No. 19 (Dob)

CARCASSI, M.

88   *Étude* [Study No. 3], Op. 60, No. 5 (FH)*
89   *Étude* [Study No. 4], Op. 60, No. 21 (FH) *

COSTE, N.

90   *Étude* [Study No. 9], Op. 38, No. 1 (FH)*

FERRER, J.

91   *Allegro moderato* [Study No. 6] (FH)*

GALLANT, P.

92   *Two-part Invention* [Study No. 10] (FH)*
93   *Chromatic Study* [Study No. 11] (FH)*

GIULIANI, M.

94   *Étude* [Study No. 5], Op. 100, No. 12 (FH)*

KOMTER, J.M.

95   *Prelude II* from *Music for Solo Guitar*, Vol. 1, No. 16 (Dob)

KRAFT, N.

96   *Study* [Study No. 7] (FH)*

SAGRERAS, J.

97   *Las cuartas lecciones*, No. 18 (Ric)
98   *Las cuartas lecciones*, No. 20 (Ric)
99   *Las cuartas lecciones*, No. 24 (Ric)
100   *Las cuartas lecciones*, No. 25 (Ric)
101   *Las cuartas lecciones*, No. 31 (Ric)
102   *Las cuartas lecciones*, No. 34 (Ric)
103   *Las quintas lecciones*, No. 1 (Ric)
104   *Las quintas lecciones*, No. 4 (Ric)
105   *Las quintas lecciones*, No. 6 (Ric)

SOR, F.

106   *Leçon* [Study No. 1], Op. 31, No. 21 (FH) *

TÁRREGA, F.

107   *Prelude* [Study No. 8], TI i-9 (FH) *

WINGFIELD, S.

108   *Interlude* [Study No. 13] (FH) *

TECHNICAL REQUIREMENTS

In preparing for the technical portion of the examination, Candidates should consult the *Royal Conservatory of Music Guitar Series: Scales and Arpeggios Album* (Oakville: Frederick Harris, 1990).

SCALES M.M. ♩ = 66

The Candidate must be prepared to play the following scales in triplet eighth notes and sixteenth notes, ascending and descending. The scales should be fingered *i m*, *m a* and *i a*, and played with free strokes and rest strokes. **Scales are NOT to be fingered as first position, openstring scales.** Follow each scale with a I-IV-V-I cadence in a four-note form. See Technical Requirements Examples, p. 51.

Major	E, B, F sharp, F, B flat—2 octaves G, A flat—3 octaves
Harmonic Minor	C sharp, G sharp, D sharp, D, G—2 octaves E, F—3 octaves
Melodic Minor	C sharp, G sharp, D sharp, D, G—2 octaves E, F—3 octaves
Chromatic	starting on C—2 octaves

SLUR SCALES M.M. ♩ = 80

Ascending and descending, compound triplet slurs.

Major . . . . D—1 octave

REPEATED-NOTE SCALES M.M. ♩ = 100

Ascending and descending in triplet eighth notes, to be fingered *i m*, rest stroke.

Major . . . . E, B, F sharp, F,
B flat—2 octaves

Harmonic Minor . . . . . . C sharp, G sharp, D sharp,
D, G—2 octaves

Melodic Minor . . . . C sharp, G sharp, D sharp,
D, G—2 octaves

SCALES IN THIRDS M.M. ♩ = 60

Ascending and descending in eighth notes, solid form.

Major . . . . C—1 octave

Harmonic Minor . . . . . . A—1 octave

SCALES IN SIXTHS M.M. ♩ = 60

Ascending and descending in eighth notes, solid form.

Major . . . . C—1 octave

Harmonic Minor . . . . . . A—1 octave

EAR TESTS

A.   RHYTHM

The Candidate will be required to sing, play or tap the rhythm of a short melody after the examiner has played it TWICE.

Time Signature: 2/4, 3/4 or 6/8

Rhythm Examples

B.   INTERVALS

The Candidate will be required:

1. to sing or hum any of the following intervals after the first note has been played ONCE by the examiner;

OR (at the choice of the Candidate)

2. to identify any of the following intervals after each has been played ONCE in broken form by the examiner:

Major 2nd, Major and Minor 3rds, Major and Minor 6ths, Perfect 4ths, 5ths and octaves Above a given note; Major and Minor 3rds, Minor 6ths, Perfect 4ths, 5ths and octaves Below a given note.

C.   MELODY PLAYBACK

The Candidate will be required to play back a melody of approximately nine notes, based on a complete major scale from tonic to tonic or from dominant to dominant, after the examiner has:

1. named the key;

2. played the tonic triad ONCE; and

3. played the melody TWICE.

The melody may begin on the tonic, mediant or dominant of C, F, G or D major.

Melody Example

D.   CHORDS

The Candidate will be required to identify the quality (Major or Minor) of any major or minor triad in root position when the chord is played ONCE by the examiner in solid form and in close position.

SIGHT READING

The Candidate will be required:

A. to play a short passage in a major or minor key equal in difficulty to a Grade 4 piece; AND

B. to clap or tap the rhythm of a melody in 3/4 or 4/4 time. In order to achieve full marks, the Candidate must maintain a steady pace and metrical accentuation. The sight reading example indicates the approximate degree of difficulty.

Sight Reading Example

THEORY CO-REQUISITE

Grade 1 Rudiments OR

Grade 2 Rudiments

GRADE SEVEN

REPERTOIRE

Candidates must be prepared to play FOUR pieces, one from each of Lists A, B, C, and D. Compositions marked * are included in the *Royal Conservatory of Music Guitar Series: Grade 7 Repertoire and Studies Album* (Oakville: Frederick Harris, 1990). Each numbered item represents one selection for examination purposes.

LIST A

CREMA, G.M. da

1 *Ricercar No. 11* (FH) *
2 *Ricercare No. 3* from *Antologia di musica antica*, Vol. 2, p. 18 (SZ; Chiesa)

DALZA, J.A.

3 *Fantasia* (Esch; Pujol)

DOWLAND, J.

4 *Melancholy Galliard*, Poulton No. 25 (FH) *

FARNABY, G.

5 *A Toye* from *Five Pieces* in GA

MILAN, L.

6 Any TWO of Nos. 2, 4, 6 from *Sei pavane* (SZ; Chiesa)
7 *Fantasia de consonances y redobles* from *Hispanae citharae ars viva* in GA

MILANO, F. da

8 *Ricercare* from *Intabolatura* (FH) *

NARVÁEZ, L. de

9 *Diferencias sobre "Guárdame las vacas"* (FH) *
10 *Canción del Emperador* (FH) *

NEUSIDLER, H.

11 *Wascha Mesa* AND *Hupff auff* from *Zwei Renaissance Stücke* in GA

LIST B

ABLONIZ, M.

12 *Preludio* AND *Gavotta* from *Partita in E Major* (Ric)

BACH, C.P.E.

13 *La Caroline*, Helm No. 98 (FH; Kraft) *

BACH, J.S.

14 *Minuets I* AND *II* from *Cello Suite No. 1*, BWV 1007 in GA
15 *Prelude*, BWV 999 (FH) *
16 *Sarabande* from *Suite in E Minor*, BWV 996 (FH) *
17 *Gavotte*, BWV 1006 in GA

BARON, E.G.

18 *Gigue* from *Music for Solo Guitar*, Vol. 1, p. 14 (Dob)

HANDEL, G.F.

19 *Fughette* AND *Air* from *Eight Aylesford Pieces* in GA

KELLNER, D.

20 *Gigue* from EGAL, Vol. 2, p. 14

PONCE, M.

21 *Courante* from *Suite* (Peer; Segovia)
22 *Gavotte I* AND *Gavotte II* from *Suite* (Peer; Segovia)

PURCELL, H.

23 *Rondo* from *Three Pieces* in GA

RONCALLI, L.

24 *Preludio* AND *Gigua* from *Neun Suiten*, No. 2 (Hof; Stingl)
25 *Preludio* AND *Gigua* from *Neun Suiten*, No. 7 (Hof; Stingl)

SANTORSOLA, G.

26 *Aria* from *Three Airs of Court* (Co)

SANZ, G.

27 *Canarios* (Wat; Mills) *

VISÉE, R. de

28 Any TWO of *Prelude, Sarabande, Menuet* from *Suite in G Minor* (SZ; Saldarelli)

WEISS, S.L.

29 *Aria* from EGAL, Vol. 2, p. 18
30 *Courante* from *Eleven Pieces*, No. 7 (Ric; Skiera)
31 *Mademoiselle Tiroloise* (FH; Kraft) *
32 *Rigaudon* from *Eleven Pieces*, No. 10 (Ric; Skiera)

LIST C

CARCASSI, M.

33 *Tempo di valse* from *Carcassi-Brevier*, Vol. 3, No. 44 in GA

COSTE, N.

34 *Berceuse* (FH) *

DIABELLI, A.

35 *Adagio* from *Drei Sonaten*, No. 2 in GA

GIULIANI, M.

36 *Allegro*, Op. 43, No. 10 (FH) *
37 *Studi per chitarra*, No. 57 (SZ; Chiesa)

GRIEG, E.

38   *Chant du paysan* from *Classical Montage* (Wat; Mills)
39   *Valse*, Op. 12, No. 2 from *Classical Montage* (Wat; Mills) *

MOZART, W.A.

40   *Menuet* in GA

PAGANINI, N.

41   *Kleine Stücke*, No. 24 (Scho; Vereczkey)

SCARLATTI, D.

42   *Sonata*, L. 238, K. 208 (FH) *
43   *Sonata*, L. 83, K. 431 from *Nine Sonatas*, Vol. 2 (Co; Lima)

SCHUMANN, R.

44   *Romanza* from *Album of Guitar Solos* (Co; Segovia)

SOR, F.

45   Any TWO of Op. 11, Nos. 1, 5, 7, 8, Op. 24, No. 1 from *Twenty Selected Minuets* in GA

TÁRREGA, F.

46   *Marieta* (FH) *
47   *La Alborada* (FH) *

LIST D

BARRIOS MANGORÉ, A.

48   *Oración por todos* from *Guitar Works*, Vol. 1, p. 14 (Belw; Stover)
49   *Preludio* from *Guitar Works*, Vol. 1, p. 12 (Belw; Stover)
50   *Gavota al estilo antiguo* from *Guitar Works*, Vol. 1, p. 18 (Belw; Stover)

BEAUVAIS, W.

51   *Jazz Waltz* (FH) *

BENEDICT, R.

52   *Divertimenti*, No. 1 (Wat)
53   *Divertimenti*, No. 8 (Wat)

BENNETT, R.R.

54   *Impromptus*, No. 5 (Uni)

BLYTON, C.   31

55   *Django Reinhardt's Stomp* from In Memoriam Django Reinhardt, Op. 64a (Berb) *

BUCZYNSKI, W.

56   *The Solitary Tree (Willow)* from *Four Corners of Gregory* (FH) *

CAMILLERI, C.

57   *Four African Sketches*, No. 4 (Cram) *

CASTELNUOVO-TEDESCO, M.

58   *Serentella* from *Appunti*, Vol. 1, No. 8 (SZ)

FALLA, M. de

59   *Récit du pêcheur* from *Two Pieces* (Ches; Pujol)

FEGGELEN, C. van

60   *Venezuelan Waltz No. 1* (FH) *

FEUERSTEIN, R.

61   *Rests and Movements* from *Three Pieces for Guitar* (Morn) *

GAGNON, C.

62   *Élegie* from *Music for Solo Guitar*, Vol. 2, No. 12 (Dob)
63   *Prelude* from *Music for Solo Guitar*, Vol. 3, p. 32 (Dob)

HARRIS, A.

64   *Aria* from *Sonatina* (Co)
65   Any TWO pieces from *Suite of Seven Pieces* (Co)

HAUG, H.

66   *Alba* (Berb; Gilardino) (FH) *

KATZ, B.

67   *You Too* (FH) *

LAURO, A.

68   *El Marabino* (Broek)
69   *Quatro valses venezolanos*, No. 1 (Broek; Diaz)
70   *Quatro valses venezolanos*, No. 2 (Broek; Diaz) *

LLOBET, M.

71   *Canco del lladre* from *Ten Catalan Folk Songs* (Uni)
72   *El nit de natal* from *Ten Catalan Folk Songs* (Uni)
73   *El noy de la mare* from *Ten Catalan Folk Songs* (Uni)
74   *El testament d'Amelia* from *Ten Catalan Folk Songs* (Uni) *
75   *Plany* from *Ten Catalan Folk Songs* (Uni)

MARSHALL, J.

76   *Afro-Cuban Lullaby* in VMG

MARTIN, F.

77   *Air* from *Quatre pièces brèves* (Uni)

32

MORENO-TORROBA, F.

78   *La Pastora* from *Aires de La Mancha* in GA

79   *Arada* from *Suite castellana* in GA (FH) *

PERRONE, J.

80   *Alma* (Per)

SEALEY, R.

81   *New York* (Wat)

SEGOVIA, A.

82   *Neblina* from *Two Pieces* (Belw)

SMITH BRINDLE, R.

83   Any TWO pieces from *Etruscan Preludes* (Scho)

84   *Nocturne* (Scho)

85   *Fuego fatuo* (Scho)

TANSMAN, A.

86   *Tempo di polonaise* from *Suite in modo polonico*, IV (Esch)

87   *Alla polacca* from *Suite in modo polonico*, VII (Esch)

88   *Sarabande* from *Cavatina* in GA

VILLA-LOBOS, H.

89   *Mazurka-Chôro* from *Suite populaire brésilienne* (Esch)

90   *Valsa-Chôro* from *Suite populaire brésilienne* (Esch)

91   *Cinq préludes*, No. 3 (Esch)

WEINZWEIG, J.

92   *Contrasts*, No. 6 (FH) *

STUDIES

Candidates must be prepared to play TWO studies of contrasting nature by different composers from the following list. Compositions marked * are included in the Studies section of the *Royal Conservatory of Music Guitar Series: Grade 7 Repertoire and Studies Album* (Oakville: Frederick Harris, 1990).

BARRIOS MANGORÉ, A.

93   *Estudio inconcluso* from *Guitar Works*, Vol. 1 (Belw; Stover)

94   *Estudio del ligado* from *Guitar Works*, Vol. 1 (Belw; Stover)

95   *Estudio en arpegio* from *Guitar Works*, Vol. 1 (Belw; Stover)

BENEDICT, R.

96   *Chromatic Fughetta 1* from *Fughettas* (Wat)

97   *Chromatic Fughetta 2* from *Fughettas* (Wat)

98   *Fughetta 3* from *Fughettas* (Wat)

BROUWER, L.

99   *Études simples*, No. 9 (Esch)

100   *Études simples*, No. 10 (Esch)

CARCASSI, MATTEO

101   *Étude* [Study No. 4], Op. 60, No. 19 (FH) *

CASTELNUOVO-TEDESCO, M.

102   *Appunti "Sulle terze"* [Study No. 5], Op. 210, Vol. 1, No. 4 (SZ) *

CHIEREGHIN, S.

103   *Preludio* [Study No. 9] (Zan; Briasco) *

COSTE, N.

104   *Twenty-five Études*, No. 2 in GA

105   *Twenty-five Études*, No. 5 in GA

106   *Twenty-five Études*, No. 6 in GA

107   *Twenty-five Études*, No. 13 in GA

DODGSON, S., and H. QUINE

108   *Prelude* from *Studies for Guitar*, Bk. 1, No. 1 (Ric)

DUKE, D.

109   *Study* [Study No. 7] (FH) *

GIULIANI, M.

110   *Studi per chitarra*, No. 48 (SZ; Chiesa)

111   *Studi per chitarra*, No. 50 (M.M. ♩ =92) (SZ; Chiesa)

112   *Studi per chitarra*, No. 51 (SZ; Chiesa)

113   *Studi per chitarra*, No. 54 (M.M. ♩ =72) (SZ; Chiesa)

114   *Studi per chitarra*, No. 55 (SZ; Chiesa)

115   *Studi per chitarra*, No. 56 (SZ; Chiesa)

116   *Studi per chitarra*, No. 57 (M.M. ♩ =69) (SZ; Chiesa)

117   *Studi per chitarra*, No. 60 (SZ; Chiesa)

HAND, F.

118   *Study No. 1* [Study No. 11] from *Five Studies* (Scho) *

KRAFT, N.

119   *Study* [Study No. 8] (FH) *

PERRONE, J.

120   *El Indio valiente* (Per)

PRESTI, I.

121   *Six Études*, No. 3 (Esch)

ROSS, C.W.

122   *Study* [Study No. 6] (FH) *

SAGRERAS, J.

123 *Las quintas lecciones*, No. 15 (Ric)
124 *Las quintas lecciones*, No. 19 (Ric)
125 *Las quintas lecciones*, No. 26 (Ric)
126 *Las quintas lecciones*, No. 30 (Ric)
127 *Las quintas lecciones*, No. 39 (Ric)
128 *Las quintas lecciones*, No. 40 (Ric)

SOR, F.

129 *Studio* [Study No. 1], Op. 6, No. 8 (FH) *
130 *Leçon* [Study No. 2], Op. 31, No. 16 (FH) *
131 *Leçon* [Study No. 3], Op. 31, No. 20 (FH) *
132 *Twenty Studies*, No. 1 (Marks; Segovia)
133 *Twenty Studies*, No. 8 (Marks; Segovia)
134 *Twenty Studies*, No. 9 (Marks; Segovia)

TÁRREGA, F.

135 *30 Original Preludes*, No. 4 [Study No. 12], TI i-4 (Ric; Piñero) *
136 *30 Original Preludes*, No. 6 [Study No. 10], TI i-6 (Ric; Piñero) *
137 *30 Original Preludes*, No. 28 (Ric; Piñero)

TECHNICAL REQUIREMENTS

In preparing for the technical portion of the examination, Candidates should consult the *Royal Conservatory of Music Guitar Series: Scales and Arpeggios Album* (Oakville: Frederick Harris, 1990).

SCALES M.M. ♩ = 80

The Candidate must be prepared to play the following scales in triplet eighth notes and sixteenth notes, ascending and descending. The scales should be fingered *i m*, *m a* and *i a*, and played with free strokes and rest strokes. **Scales are NOT to be fingered as first position, open-string scales.** Follow each scale with a I-IV-V-I cadence in a four-note form. See Technical Requirements Examples, p. 51.

Major . . . . all keys—2 octaves
                            A, E, F—3 octaves

Harmonic Minor . . . . . . all keys—2 octaves
                            F sharp—3 octaves

Melodic Minor . . . . all keys—2 octaves
                            F sharp—3 octaves

Chromatic . . . . starting on G—2 octaves

SLUR SCALES M.M. ♩ = 104

Ascending and descending, compound triplet slurs.

Major . . . . G—1 octave

REPEATED NOTE SCALES M.M. ♩ = 80

Ascending and descending, in quintuplets, to be fingered *i m*.

Major . . . . all keys—2 octaves

Harmonic Minor . . . . . . all keys—2 octaves

Melodic Minor . . . . . . all keys—2 octaves

SCALES IN THIRDS M.M. ♩ = 66

Ascending and descending, in eighth notes, solid form.

Major . . . . G—1 octave

Harmonic Minor . . . . . . E—1 octave

SCALES IN SIXTHS M.M. ♩ = 66

Ascending and descending, in eighth notes, solid form.

Major . . . . G—1 octave

Harmonic Minor . . . . . . E—1 octave

CHORDAL SCALES M.M. ♩ = 56

Ascending and descending, in eighth notes, solid form.

Major . . . . G—1 octave

Harmonic Minor . . . . . . E—1 octave

EAR TESTS

A. RHYTHM

The Candidate will be required to sing, play or tap the rhythm of a short melody after the examiner has played it TWICE.

Time Signature: 2/4, 3/4 or 6/8

See rhythm examples for the approximate degree of difficulty.

Rhythm Examples

B. INTERVALS

The Candidate will be required:

1. to sing or hum any of the following intervals after the first note has been played ONCE by the examiner;

OR (at the choice of the Candidate)

2. to identify any of the following intervals after each has been played ONCE in broken form by the examiner:

Major and Minor 2nds, 3rds and 6ths, Perfect 4ths, 5ths and octaves Above a given note; Major and Minor 3rds, Minor 6ths, Major 7ths, Perfect 4ths, 5ths and octaves Below a given note.

34

C.   MELODY   PLAYBACK

The Candidate will be required to play back a melody of approximately nine notes, based on a complete major scale from tonic to tonic, mediant to mediant, or dominant to dominant, after the examiner has:

1. named the key;

2. played the tonic triad ONCE; and

3. played the melody TWICE.

The melody may begin on the tonic, mediant, dominant or upper tonic of C, G, D, F or B flat major. See the melody example for the approximate degree of difficulty.

Melody Example

D.   CHORDS

The Candidate will be required to identify the quality (Major or Minor) and type (triad or dominant seventh) of any major or minor triad or dominant seventh chord in root position when the chord is played ONCE in solid form and in close position by the examiner.

SIGHT READING

The Candidate will be required:

A. to play a short passage in a major or minor key equal in difficulty to a Grade 5 piece; AND

B. to clap or tap the rhythm of a melody in 2/4 or 6/8 time. In order to achieve full marks, the Candidate must maintain a steady pace and metrical accentuation. The sight reading example indicates the approximate degree of difficulty.

Sight Reading Example

THEORY CO-REQUISITE

Grade 2 Rudiments

GRADE EIGHT

REPERTOIRE

Candidates must be prepared to play FOUR pieces, one from each of Lists A, B, C, and D. Compositions marked * are included in the *Royal Conservatory of Music Guitar Series: Grade 8 Repertoire and Studies Album* (Oakville: Frederick Harris, 1990). Each numbered item represents one selection for examination purposes.

LIST A

BESARD, J.B.

1 *Bergamasco* from *Scelta di brani*, Vol. II, p. 4 (Ric)

DOWLAND, J.

2 *Allemande*, Poulton No. 54 (FH) *
3 *Come Heavy Sleep* from *First Book of Airs* (FH; Kraft) *
4 *Queen Elizabeth, Her Galliard*, Poulton No. 41 (FH) *

HOVE, J. van den

5 *Praeludium* from EGAL, Vol. 6, p. 12

MUDARRA, A.

6 *Diferencias sobre "Conde Claros"* (FH) *
7 *Romanesca I, Guárdame las vacas* in GA

SWEELINCK, J.P.

8 *Fantasia* from EGAL, Vol. 6, p. 18

LIST B

BACH, J.S.

9 *Allemande* from *Lute Suite No. 1*, BWV 996 *
10 *Andante* from *Violin Sonata*, BWV 1003 (Co; Lima)
11 *Gavottes I AND II* from *Lute Suite*, BWV 995
12 *Minuets I AND II* from *Lute Partita*, BWV 1006a
13 *Prelude* from *Violoncello Suite*, BWV 1007 (FH; Kraft) *
14 *Sarabande* from *Violoncello Suite*, BWV 1009 *
15 *Sarabande* from *Lute Partita*, BWV 997
16 *Siciliana* from *Violin Sonata*, BWV 1001 (Nov; Duarte)

CIMAROSA, D.

17 *Three Sonatas* (Fab; Bream), *Nos. 1 AND 3*

FROBERGER, J.J.

18 *Giga* from *I bis del concertista*, Vol. 2, p. 1 (SZ; Chiesa)

SCARLATTI, D.

19 *Sonata*, L. 483, K. 322 (FH) *
20 *Sonata*, L. 352 from *Nine Sonatas*, Vol. 1 (Co; Lima)

VISÉE, R. de

21 Any THREE of *Prelude, Allemande, Courante, Gavotte, Gigue* from *Suite in D Minor* (Ric; Paolini)
22 *Le tombeau de François Corbetta* (Esch; Pujol)

WEISS, S.L.

23 *Courante* from *Intavolatura di liuto, Suite VIII* in *Six Lute Pieces*, Vol. 2

LIST C

AGUADO, D.

24 *Menuett I* from *Aguado-Brevier* in GA
25 *Menuett II* from *Aguado-Brevier* in GA
26 *Menuett III* from *Aguado-Brevier* in GA
27 *Andante I* from *Aguado-Brevier* in GA

CARULLI, F.

28 *Sonata I* from *Drei Sonaten* in GA
29 *Sonata II* from *Drei Sonaten* in GA
30 *Sonata III* from *Drei Sonaten* in GA
31 *Sei Andanti*, Op. 320, No. 1 (SZ; Chiesa)
32 *Sei Andanti*, Op. 320, No. 2 (SZ; Chiesa)

DIABELLI, A.

33 *Andante sostenuto* from *Sonata in A Major* (Fab; Bream)
34 *Minuetto* from *Sonata in A Major* (Fab; Bream)

GIULIANI, M.

35 *Adagio* from *Sonata*, Op. 15 (FH) *
36 *Giulianate*, Op. 148, No. 2 (SZ; Chiesa)
37 *Giulianate*, Op. 148, No. 3 (SZ; Chiesa)
38 *Giulianate*, Op. 148, No. 4 (SZ; Chiesa)
39 *Giulianate*, Op. 148, No. 5 (SZ; Chiesa)
40 *Giulianate*, Op. 148, No. 6 (SZ; Chiesa)
41 *Giulianate*, Op. 148, No. 7 (SZ; Chiesa)
42 *Rondo in A Major*, Op. 17, No. 1 in GA
43 *Rondo in G Major*, Op. 8, No. 2 in GA

GRIEG, E.

44 *Melody*, Op. 38, No. 3 from *Album of Guitar Solos* (Co; Segovia)

HAYDN, J.

45 *Menuett* from *Quartet in G Major*, Hob. III, 75 in GA

MOZART, W.A.

46 *Allegro* from *Larghetto and Allegro*, K. Anh. 229 (Fab; Bream)
47 *Larghetto* from *Larghetto and Allegro*, K. Anh. 229 (Fab; Bream)

PAGANINI, N.

48 *Romance* from *Grand Sonata*, M.S. No. 3 (FH; Kraft) *

36

PONCE, M.

49   *Andante* from *Sonata clásica* in GA

50   *Menuet* AND *Trio* from *Sonata clásica* in GA

SCHUMANN, R.

51   *Kindersonaten*, Op. 118, No. 1 (Fab; Bream)

52   *Kindersonaten*, Op. 118, No. 2 (Fab; Bream)

53   *Kindersonaten*, Op. 118, No. 3 (Fab; Bream)

SOR, F.

54   *Andante largo*, Op. 5, No. 5 (Uni; Scheit)

55   *Folies d'Espagne*, Op. 15, No. 1 in *Antologia* (Ric; Savio)

56   *Largo* from *Fantasia No. 1*, Op. 7 (FH) *

57   *Fantasia No. 2*, Op. 4 (Ox; Quine)

58   *Rondo in C*, Op. 22 (FH)

59   *Minuets*, Op. 11, Nos. 6 AND 10 in *Twenty Selected Minuets* in GA

TÁRREGA, F.

60   *Mazurca en sol* from *Doce composiciones* (Ric; Savio) *

LIST D

BARRIOS MANGORÉ, A.

61   *Allegro* from *La Catedral* (Zan) (Belw)

62   *Primavera-vals* from *Guitar Works*, Vol. 1 (Belw; Stover)

63   *Julia Florida* (Belw) (FH) *

BENEDICT, R.

64   *Old Fugue* from *Fughettas* (Wat)

BROUWER, L.

65   *Danza característica* in GA

66   *Guajira* AND *Zapateo* from *Dos aires populares cubanos* (Esch)

CASTELNUOVO-TEDESCO, M.

67   *A Platero en el cielo de Moguer* from *Platero y yo*, Vol. 4, Op. 190 (Berb; Gilardino) *

68   *Valse française* from *Appunti*, Op. 210, Vol. 3, No. 14 (SZ; Chiesa)

CHIEREGHIN, S.

69   *Danza* from *Sotto tenero verde* (Zan) *

DEBUSSY, C.

70   *The Little Shepherd* in VMG

DODGSON, S.

71   *Adagio* from *Partita I for Guitar* (Ox) *

DUARTE, J.

72   *Prelude* from *English Suite*, Op. 31 (Nov)

73   Any TWO Movements from *Sonatinette* (Nov)

FEGGELEN, C. van

74   *Chôro II* (FH)

FEUERSTEIN, R.

75   *Flight* (Morn) *

HAUG, H.

76   *Preludio* (Berb)

JAMIESON, D.

77   *Adagio* from *Sonata* (FH)

KOVATS, B.

78   Any THREE of *Andantino, Leggiero, Molto legando, Moderato, Un poco agitato, Non troppo allegro, Tranquillamente scorrendo, Vivo, Ritmico* from *Minutenstücke* in GA

LAURO, A.

79   *Vals venezolano No. 3* from *Quatro valses venezolanos* (Broek; Diaz) *

MOMPOU, F.

80   *Cuna* from *Suite compostelana* (Sal)

81   *Canción* from *Suite compostelana* (Sal)

MORENO-TORROBA, F.

82   *Albada* from *Pièces caractéristiques*, Vol. 2 in GA

83   *Danza* from *Suite castellana* in GA

84   *Fandanguillo* from *Suite castellana* in GA

85   *Los Mayos* from *Pièces caractéristiques*, Vol. 2 in GA

86   *Andante* from *Sonatina* (Co; Segovia)

87   *Serenata burlesca* in GA

MUSSORGSKY, M.

88   *The Old Castle* from *Pictures at an Exhibition* (Wat; Mills) *

MYERS, S.

89   *Cavatina* (Robb; Williams)

PENNYCOOK, B.

90   *Finale* from *August Suite* (FH) *

PERRONE, J.

91   *Vaya con Juan* (Per)

PETIT, P.

92   *Nocturne* (Esch)

PONCE, M.

93 *Chanson* from *Sonata III* in GA (Segovia) *

94 *Tres canciones populares mexicanas*, Nos. 2 AND 3 in GA

95 *Scherzino mexicano* (Peer; Lopez-Ramos)

96 *Twelve Preludes*, Vol. 1, Nos. 1 AND 2 in GA

97 *Twelve Preludes*, Vol. 1, Nos. 3 AND 4 in GA

98 *Twelve Preludes*, Vol. 2, Nos. 7 AND 8 in GA

SAINZ DE LA MAZA, R.

99 *El vito* (UME)

SEGOVIA, A.

100 *Estudio sin luz* in GA

SMITH BRINDLE, R.

101 *Do Not Go Gentle* (SZ)

SOMERS, H.

102 *Finale* from *Sonata* (Cav)

TANSMAN, A.

103 *Danza pomposa* in GA

VILLA-LOBOS, H.

104 *Schottisch-Chôro* from *Suite populaire brésilienne*, No. 2 (Esch)

105 *Gavotta-Chôro* from *Suite populaire brésilienne*, No. 4 (Esch)

106 *Chôro-Typico* (Co)

107 *Cinq préludes*, No. 3 (Esch)

WEINZWEIG, J.

108 *Contrasts*, No. 2 (CMC)

WILSON, D.

109 *Autumn Elegy* (FH) *

STUDIES

Candidates must be prepared to play TWO studies of contrasting nature by different composers from the following list. Compositions marked * are included in the Studies section of the *Royal Conservatory of Music Guitar Series: Grade 8 Repertoire and Studies Album* (Oakville: Frederick Harris, 1990).

CARCASSI, M.

110 *Étude* [Study No. 5] from *25 études mélodiques*, Op. 60, No. 20 (FH) *

CASTELNUOVO-TEDESCO, M.

111 *Sulle seconde* [Study No. 6] from *Appunti*, Op. 210, Vol. 1, No. 3 (SZ; Chiesa) *

CHIEREGHIN, S.

112 *Studio* [Study No. 7] from *Invenzione Leid e Studio* (FH) *

COSTE, N.

113 *Twenty-five Études*, No.7 in GA

GALLANT, P.

114 *Adieu* [Study No. 9] (EGF) *

GIULIANI, M.

115 *Étude* [Study No. 3] from *Études instructives*, Op. 100, No. 11 (FH) *

PERRONE, J.

116 *Los jinetes* (Per)

PUJOL, E.

117 *El Abejorro* (Ric)

PRESTI, I.

118 *Six Études*, No. 1 (Esch)

119 *Six Études*, No. 2 (Esch)

SAGRERAS, J.

120 *Las quintas lecciones*, No. 24 (Ric)

SOR, F.

121 *Exercice* [Study No. 4] from *24 exercices*, Op. 35, No. 16 (FH) *

122 *Leçon* [Study No. 2] from *24 leçons*, Op. 31, No. 19 (FH) *

123 *Studio* [Study No. 1] from *Studio for the Spanish Guitar*, Op. 6, No. 11 (FH) *

TÁRREGA, F.

124 *Prelude No. 15* [Study No. 8], TI ii-4b (FH) *

VILLA-LOBOS, H.

125 *Douze études*, No. 1 (Esch)

126 *Douze études*, No. 8 (Esch)

127 *Douze études*, No. 11 (Esch)

TECHNICAL REQUIREMENTS

In preparing for the technical portion of the examination, Candidates should consult the *Royal Conservatory of Music Guitar Series: Scales and Arpeggios Album* (Oakville: Frederick Harris, 1990).

SCALES M.M. ♩ = 96

The Candidate must be prepared to play the following scales in triplet eighth notes and sixteenth notes, ascending and descending. The scales should be fingered *i m*, *m a* and *i a*, and played with free strokes and rest strokes. **Scales are NOT to be fingered as first position, open-string scales.** Follow each scale with a I-IV-V-I cadence in a four-note form. See Technical Requirements Examples, p. 51.

Major . . . . all keys—2 and 3 octaves
where possible

Harmonic Minor . . . . . . all keys—2 and 3 octaves
where possible

Melodic Minor . . . . all keys—2 and 3 octaves
where possible

Chromatic . . . . starting on E flat—2 octaves

SLUR SCALES M.M. ♩ = 116

Ascending and descending, compound triplet slurs.

Major . . . . C, A—1 octave

REPEATED NOTE SCALES M.M. ♩ = 80

Ascending and descending in sextuplets, to be fingered
i m, rest stroke.

Major . . . . all keys—2 octaves

Harmonic Minor . . . . . . all keys—2 octaves

Melodic Minor . . . . . . all keys—2 octaves

SCALES IN THIRDS M.M. ♩ = 80

Ascending and descending solid form in eighth notes,
broken form in sixteenths.

Major . . . . D—2 octaves

Harmonic Minor . . . . . . B—2 octaves

SCALES IN SIXTHS M.M. ♩ = 80

Ascending and descending solid form in eighth notes,
broken form in sixteenths.

Major . . . . D—2 octaves

Harmonic Minor . . . . . . B—2 octaves

CHORDAL SCALES M.M. ♩ = 66

Ascending and descending solid form in eighth notes,
broken form in triplet sixteenths.

Major . . . . D—1 octave

Harmonic Minor . . . . . . B—1 octave

EAR TESTS

A. INTERVALS

The Candidate will be required:

1. to sing or hum any of the following intervals after the
first note has been played ONCE by the examiner;

OR (at the choice of the Candidate)

2. to identify any of the following intervals after each has
been played ONCE in broken form by the examiner:

**Major and Minor 2nds, 3rds, 6ths, Minor 7ths, Perfect
4ths, 5ths and octaves Above a given note; Major 2nds,
Major and Minor 3rds, Minor 6ths, Major 7ths, Perfect
4ths, 5ths and octaves Below a given note.**

B. MELODY PLAYBACK

The Candidate will be required to play back a melody of
approximately nine notes, within the range of an octave
and comprised of rhythmic figures slightly in advance of
the rhythmic test (A) of the previous grade, after the
examiner has:

1. named the key;

2. played the tonic triad ONCE; and

3. played the melody TWICE.

The melody may be in the key of C, G, D, F or B flat
major.

Melody Example

C. CHORDS

The Candidate will be required to identify the quality
(Major or Minor) and type (triad, dominant 7th or
diminished 7th) of any major or minor triad and any
dominant and diminished 7th chord in root position
when the chord is played ONCE by the examiner in
solid form and in close position.

D. CADENCES

The Candidate will be required to identify by name or
symbols any of the following cadences after the examiner
has played the tonic chord ONCE, and then has TWICE
played a short phrase in a major or minor key ending
with a cadence.

Perfect (Authentic or V-I) and Plagal (IV-I).

Cadence Example

SIGHT READING

The Candidate will be required:

A. to play a short passage equal in difficulty to a Grade
6 piece; AND

B. to clap or tap the rhythm of a melody in 3/4 or 6/8 time.
In order to achieve full marks, the Candidate must maintain a steady pace and metrical accentuation. The sight
reading example indicates the approximate degree of difficulty of the melody.

Sight Reading Example

THEORY CO-REQUISITE

Grade 2 Rudiments

GRADE NINE

REPERTOIRE

Candidates must be prepared to play FOUR pieces, one from each of Lists A, B, C, and D. Each numbered item represents one selection for examination purposes.

LIST A

BACH, J.S.

1 Allemande from Lute Suite, BWV 995 (Ric; Teuchert)
2 Bourrées I AND II from Cello Suite, BWV 1009 in GA
3 Gigue from Lute Suite, BWV 995 (Ric; Teuchert)
4 Prelude from Prelude, Fugue and Allegro in E flat for Lute, BWV 998 in GA
5 Prelude from Cello Suite, BWV 1009 in GA

BUXTEHUDE, D.

6 Any TWO of Allemande, Courante, Gigue from Suite in E Minor (Fab; Bream)

CIMAROSA, D.

7 Sonata No. 2 from Three Sonatas (Fab; Bream)
8 Sonata No. 15 (Co; Artzt)

DOWLAND, J.

9 Fantasia, Poulton No. 5 from Varietie of Lute Lessons, Vol. IV (Berb; Duarte & Poulton)
10 Farewell Fantasia, Poulton No. 3 from Varietie of Lute Lessons, Vol. IV (Berb; Duarte & Poulton)
11 Lachrimae, Poulton No. 15 from Dances & Fantasies (EMB; Benko)
12 Lady Rich, Her Galliard from Varietie of Lute Lessons, Vol. V (Berb; Duarte & Poulton)

FRESCOBALDI, G.

13 Aria con variazioni (FH; Kraft)

HANDEL, G.F.

14 Sarabanda with variations, HWV 437/4 from I bis del concertista, Vol. II (SZ; Chiesa)

MUDARRA, A.

15 Fantasia X from Two Fantasies/Two Tientos (Ric; Paolini)

PONCE, M.

16 Prelude in E (Beran)

SCARLATTI, D.

17 Sonata, L. 395, K. 533 from Three Sonatas (Co; Lima)

WEISS, S.L.

18 Chaconne from Six Lute Pieces, Vol. 2 (Co; Lima)
19 Ciacona (Co; Artzt)
20 Fantasie (Uni; Scheit)
21 Passacaglia (Uni; Scheit)
22 Tombeau sur la mort de M. Comte de Logy (Uni; Scheit)

LIST B

AGUADO, D.

23 Andantes II AND III from Selected Pieces in GA

ALBÉNIZ, M.

24 Sonata (Co; Cochran)

CARULLI, F.

25 Rondo from Selected Works for Guitar, Vol. 3, No. 59 in GA
26 Sei andanti, Op. 320, No. 3 (SZ; Chiesa)
27 Sei andanti, Op. 320, No. 5 (SZ; Chiesa)
28 Sei andanti, Op. 320, No. 6 (SZ; Chiesa)

DIABELLI, A.

29 Rondo from Sonata in A Major (Fab; Bream)

GIULIANI, M.

30 Any Two Movements of Sonatina, Op. 71, No. 2 from Compositions for Guitar, Vol. 1 (Ric; Savio)
31 Andantino AND Finale from Sonatinas, Op. 71, No. 3 (SZ; Chiesa)
32 La risoluzione from Giulianate, Op. 148, No. 1 (SZ; Chiesa)
33 First Movement from Sonata, Op. 15 (SZ; Chiesa)
34 Third Movement from Sonata, Op. 15 (SZ; Chiesa)
35 Variazioni su "Il Flauto Magico" di Mozart, WoO G-3 from Tre temi favoriti (Ric; Cavazzoli)
36 Variazioni sul tema della Follia di Spagna, Op. 45 (SZ; Chiesa)

HAYDN, F.J.

37 Menuetto in D, MIN [400] (UME; Segovia)

SOR, F.

38 First Movement from Sonata, Op. 22 in Nineteen Compositions (Ric; Savio)
39 Sonata, Op. 15, No. 2 from Nineteen Compositions (Ric; Savio)

LIST C

ALBÉNIZ, I.

40 Asturias from Suite española, Op. 181, No. 5 (Ric; Segovia)
41 Cadíz from Suite española, Op. 181, No. 4 (Belw; Barrueco)
42 Granada from Suite española, Op. 181, No. 1 (Belw; Barrueco)
43 Tango from España, Op. 165, No. 2 in GA

40

BARRIOS MANGORÉ, A.

44 *Canción de cuna* from *Guitar Works*, Vol. 2 (Belw; Stover)
45 *Canción de la hilandera* from *Guitar Works*, Vol. 2
      (Belw; Stover)
46 *Chôro de Saudade* (B; Cimma)
47 *Danza paraguaya* from *Guitar Works*, Vol. 3 (Belw; Stover)
48 *La catedral* from *Guitar Works*, Vol. 3 (Belw; Stover)
49 *Preludio*, Op. 5, No. 1 (Ric)

CASTELNUOVO-TEDESCO, M.

50 *Mélancolia* from *Platero y yo*, Op. 190, Vol. 1 (B; Gilardino)

DEBUSSY, C.

51 *La fille aux cheveux de lin* from *Préludes pour piano*, Bk. 1,
      No. 8 (Wat; Kraft)

FALLA, M. de

52 *Homenaje* (JMC; Duarte)

GRANADOS, E.

53 *Danza española*, No. 5 (Wat; Kraft)
54 *Fandango* from *Two Spanish Dances*, No. 3 (Co; Lima)

LAURO, A.

55 *Variations on a Venezolean Children's Song* (Broek; Diaz)

MOMPOU, F.

56 *Muñeira* from *Suite compostellana* (Sal)
57 *Preludio* from *Suite compostellana* (Sal)

MORENO-TORROBA, F.

58 Any TWO of *Jeringonza, Coplilla, Seguidilla* from
      Aires de La Mancha in GA
59 *Madroños* (Assoc)
60 *Nocturno* in GA
61 *Oliveras* from *Pièces caractéristiques*, Vol. 1 in GA

RODRIGO, J.

62 *En los trigales* (EMM; Yepes)

SAINZ DE LA MAZA, E.

63 *Campañas del alba* (UME)

SANTÓRSOLA, G.

64 *Preludio* AND *Finale* from *Three Airs of Court* (Co)

TÁRREGA, F.

65 *Capricho árabe, serenata*
66 *Estudio, TI ii-9* (*Recuerdos de la Alhambra*)

TURINA, J.

67 *Garrotin* from *Hommage à Tárrega* in GA
68 *Soleares* from *Hommage à Tárrega* in GA
69 *Ráfaga* in GA

VILLA-LOBOS, H.

70 *Cinq préludes*, No. 2 (Esch)
71 *Cinq préludes*, No. 5 (Esch)

LIST D

BALADA, L.

72 *Moderato* AND *Andantino* from *Suite No. 1* (Co)

BROUWER, L.

73 *Elogio de la danza* in GA
74 Any TWO movements from *Tres apuntes* in GA

DUARTE, J.

75 *Idylle pour IDA* (Uni)

HARRIS, A.

76 *Homage to Unamuno* (Co)

MAXWELL-DAVIES, P.

77 *Lullaby for Ilian Rainbow* (Boo)

MILHAUD, D.

78 *Segoviana* (H)

PERRONE, J.

79 *Estudio* (Per)

PRESTI, I.

80 *Étude du matin* (Co)

SMITH BRINDLE, R.

81 Any TWO Movements from *Sonata No. 3* (Scho)
82 Any TWO Movements from *Sonata No. 4* (Scho)
83 *El Polifemo de oro* (Scho)
84 *November Memories* (SZ)

VIVIER, C.

85 *Pour guitare* (Dob)

WALTON, W.

86 *Five Bagatelles*, Nos. 3 AND 4 (Ox; Bream)

WILSON, D.

87 Any TWO pieces from *Three Pieces* (B; Gilardino)

STUDIES

Candidates must be prepared to play TWO studies of contrasting nature by different composers from the following list:

AGUADO, D.

88   *Studi per chitarra*, No. 49 (SZ; Chiesa)
89   *Studi per chitarra*, No. 50 (SZ; Chiesa)

BARRIOS MANGORÉ, A.

90   *Estudio No. 3* from *Guitar Works*, Vol. 2 (Belw; Stover)

CASTELNUOVO-TEDESCO, M.

91   *Appunti*, Vol. 1, No. 10 (SZ)
92   *Appunti*, Vol. 1, No. 11 (SZ)

CARCASSI, M.

93   *Twenty-five Melodic and Progressive Studies*, No. 25 (Ric; Margaria)

COSTE, N.

94   *Twenty-five Études*, Op. 38, No. 8 in GA
95   *Twenty-five Études*, Op. 38, No. 11 in GA
96   *Twenty-five Études*, Op. 38, No. 17 in GA
97   *Twenty-five Études*, Op. 38, No. 18 in GA
98   *Twenty-five Études*, Op. 38, No. 25 in GA

DODGSON, S. and H. QUINE

99   *Studies*, Vol. 1, No. 4 (Ric)
100   *Studies*, Vol. 2, No. 14 (Ric)
101   *Studies*, Vol. 2, No. 15 (Ric)

GIULIANI, M.

102   *Studi per chitarra*, No. 65 (SZ; Chiesa)
103   *Studi per chitarra*, No. 79 (SZ; Chiesa)

LAGOYA, A.

104   *Six Études*, No. 2 (Esch)
105   *Six Études*, No. 6 (Esch)

PRESTI, I.

106   *Six Études*, No. 4 (Esch)
107   *Six Études*, No. 5 (Esch)

SOR, F.

108   *Twenty Studies*, No. 11 (Op. 29, No. 10) (Marks; Segovia)
109   *Twenty Studies*, No. 14 (Op. 31, No. 19) (Marks; Segovia)
110   *Twenty Studies*, No. 16 (Op. 31, No. 21) (Marks; Segovia)
111   *Twenty Studies*, No. 19 (Op. 35, No. 17) (Marks; Segovia)

VILLA-LOBOS, H.

112   *Douze études*, No. 4 (Esch)
113   *Douze études*, No. 6 (Esch)

TECHNICAL REQUIREMENTS

In preparing for the technical portion of the examination, Candidates should consult the *Royal Conservatory of Music Guitar Series: Scales and Arpeggios Album* (Oakville: Frederick Harris, 1990).

SCALES M.M. ♩ = 108

The Candidate must be prepared to play the following scales in triplet eighth notes and sixteenth notes, ascending and descending. The scales should be fingered *i m*, *m a*, *i a* and any *i m a* combination of the Candidate's choosing, and played with free strokes and rest strokes. **Scales are NOT to be fingered as first position, open-string scales.** Follow each scale with a I-IV-V-I cadence in a four-note form. See Technical Requirements Examples, p. 51.

Major	all keys—2 and 3 octaves where possible
Harmonic Minor	all keys—2 and 3 octaves where possible
Melodic Minor	all keys—2 and 3 octaves where possible
Chromatic	starting on E—3 octaves

SLUR SCALES M.M. ♩ = 132

Ascending and descending, compound triplet slurs.

Major	G, A—2 octaves

REPEATED-NOTE SCALES

Ascending and descending in triplets and quadruplets (M.M. ♩ = 112); in quintuplets and sextuplets (M.M ♩ = 76), to be fingered *i m*, *m a*, *i a*, and any other *i m a* combination; rest strokes throughout.

Major	all keys—2 octaves
Harmonic	all keys—2 octaves
Melodic Minor	all keys—2 octaves

SCALES IN THIRDS M.M. ♩ = 88

Ascending and descending solid form in eighth notes, broken form in sixteenths.

Major	A—2 octaves
Harmonic Minor	F sharp—2 octaves

SCALES IN SIXTHS M.M. ♩ = 88

Ascending and descending solid form in eighth notes, broken form in sixteenths.

Major	A—2 octaves
Harmonic Minor	F sharp—2 octaves

CHORDAL SCALES M.M. ♩ = 76

Ascending and descending solid form in eighth notes, broken form in triplet sixteenths.

Major . . . . A—1 octave

Harmonic Minor . . . . . . F sharp—1 octave

EAR TESTS

A. INTERVALS

The Candidate will be required:

1. to sing or hum any of the following intervals after the first note has been played ONCE by the examiner;

OR (at the choice of the Candidate)

2. to identify any of the following intervals after each has been played ONCE in broken form by the examiner:

All intervals within the octave Above and Below a given note.

B. MELODY PLAYBACK

The Candidate will be required to play back the upper voice of a two-part phrase in a major key, after the examiner has:

1. named the key;

2. played the tonic chord ONCE; and

3. played the phrase TWICE.

Melody Example

C. CHORDS

The Candidate will be required to identify:

A. the quality (Major or Minor), and inversion (first inversion or root position) of any major or minor triad in root position or first inversion; AND

B. the type (triad, dominant 7th or diminished 7th) of any major or minor triad, dominant or diminished 7th chord in root position when the chord is played ONCE by the examiner in solid form and in close position.

D. CADENCES

The Candidate will be required to identify by name or symbols any of the following cadences after the examiner has played the tonic chord ONCE, and then has TWICE played a short phrase in a major or minor key ending with a cadence.

Perfect (Authentic or V-I), Imperfect (I-V) and Plagal (IV-I).

Cadence Example

SIGHT READING

The Candidate will be required:

A. to play a short passage equal in difficulty to a Grade 7 piece; AND

B. to clap or tap the rhythm of a melody in 3/4 or 4/4 time. In order to achieve full marks, the Candidate must maintain a steady pace and metrical accentuation. The sight reading example indicates the approximate degree of difficulty of the melody.

Sight Reading Example

THEORY CO-REQUISITES

Grade 2 Rudiments

Grade 3 Harmony or Introductory Keyboard Harmony

Grade 3 History

GRADE TEN

REPERTOIRE

Candidates must be prepared to play FIVE pieces, one from each of Lists A, B, C, D and E. Each numbered item represents one selection for examination purposes.

LIST A

DOWLAND, J.

1   *Sir Henry Guilford, His Almaine* from *Varietie of Lute Lessons*, Vol. II (B; Duarte-Poulton)
2   *Sir John Smith, His Almaine* from *Varietie of Lute Lessons*, Vol. II (B; Duarte-Poulton)
3   *Fantasia No. 6* from *Varietie of Lute Lessons*, Vol. IV (B; Duarte-Poulton)
4   *Fantasia No. 7* from *Varietie of Lute Lessons*, Vol. IV (B; Duarte-Poulton)
5   *Earl of Essex, His Galliard* from *Varietie of Lute Lessons*, Vol. V (B; Duarte-Poulton)

MILANO, F. da

6   *Fantasia*, in *Antologia di musica antica*, Vol. 1, p. 7 (SZ; Chiesa)

PONCE, M.

7   *Preambule* AND *Allegro vivo* from *Suite* (Peer)

SCARLATTI, D.

8   *Sonata*, L. 23, K. 380 (B; Luconi)

WEISS, S.L.

9   Any TWO of *Allemande, Courante, Giga* from *Suite No. 2* in *Intavolatura di liuto*, Vol. 1 (SZ; Chiesa)
10 Any TWO of *Allemande, Courante, Gigue* from *Suite No. 8* in *Intavolatura di liuto*, Vol. 1 (SZ; Chiesa)
11 *Allemande* AND *Pastorrel* from *Suite No. 12* in *Intavolatura di liuto*, Vol. 1 (SZ; Chiesa)
12 *Ouverture* AND *Gigue* from *Suite No. 20* in *Intavolatura di liuto*, Vol. 2 (SZ)
13 *Entree* AND *Courante* from *Suite No. 25* in *Intavolatura di liuto*, Vol. 2 (SZ)

LIST B

BACH, J.S.

14 *Fugue for Lute*, BWV 1000
15 *Allemande* AND *Courante* from *Cello Suite No. 1*, BWV 1007
16 *Allemande* AND *Courante* from *Cello Suite No. 3*, BWV 1009
17 *Prelude, Presto* AND *Courante* from *Lute Suite No. 1*, BWV 995
18 *Prelude, Presto* AND *Double* from *Lute Suite No. 2*, BWV 996
19 *Loure* AND *Gavotte* from *Lute Suite No. 4*, BWV 1006a

LIST C

GIULIANI, M.

20 *Variazioni*, Op. 112 (SZ; Chiesa)
21 *Variazioni su un tema di Handel*, Op. 107 (SZ; Chiesa)

SOR, F.

22 *Theme and Variations* from *Fantasia No. 1*, Op. 7 (Ox; Quine)
23 *Theme and Variations* from *Fantasia No. 3*, Op. 10 (Ox; Quine)
24 *Variations on "O Cara Armonia"* by Mozart, Op. 9 in GA
25 *Andantino grazioso* from *Sonata*, Op. 25 (Ric; Segovia)

TOROK, A.

26 *Variations on a Classic Theme* (Wat)

LIST D

ALBÉNIZ, I.

27 *Torre Bermeja* (Wat; Kraft)
28 *Sevilla* (Wat; Kraft)
29 *Córdoba* (Co; Lima)
30 *Mallorca* (Co; Segovia)
31 *Zambra granadina* (Co; Segovia)

CASTELNUOVO-TEDESCO, M.

32 *Tarantella* (Ric)
33 *Preludio* from *Suite in GA*
34 *Capriccio* from *Suite in GA*
35 *El Canario* from *Escarraman*, Op. 177 (Berb)

GRANADOS, E.

36 *La maja de Goya* (UME; Llobet)
37 *Danza española No. 10* (UME; Llobet)

MALATS, J.

38 *Serenata spagnola* from *I bis del concertista*, Vol. II, p. 15 (SZ; Tonazzi)

MERTZ, J.K.

39 *Tarantelle* (Presser; Leisner)

MORENO-TORROBA, F.

40 *Allegretto* from *Sonatina* (Co; Segovia)
41 *Allegro* from *Sonatina* (Co; Segovia)

PONCE, M.

42 *First Movement* from *Sonatina meridional* in GA
43 *First Movement* from *Sonata clásica* in GA
44 *Fourth Movement* from *Sonata clásica* in GA

44

PUJOL, E.

45 *Tango* from *Trois morceaux espagnols* (Esch)
46 *Guajira* from *Trois morceaux espagnols* (Esch)

RODRIGO, J.

47 *Fandango* from *Tres piezas españolas* in GA
48 *Passacaglia* from *Tres piezas españolas* in GA

TURINA, J.

49 *Fandanguillo* in GA
50 *First Movement* from *Sonata* in GA
51 *Third Movement* from *Sonata* in GA

LIST E

APIVOR, D.

52 Any THREE Movements from *Discanti*, Op. 48 (Berb)

BALADA, L.

53 Any TWO of *Allegretto, Lento, Animado* from *Suite No. 1* (Co; Lima)
54 *Lento with Variation* (Co; Lima)

BENNETT, R.R.

55 *Impromptus I, II AND IV* (Uni)

BERKELEY, L.

56 Any TWO Movements from *Sonatina* (Ches; Bream)
57 *Theme and Variations* (Ches; Gilardino)

BROUWER, L.

58 *Canticum* in GA
59 *La espiral eterna* in GA

DODGSON, S.

60 *Étude-Caprice* (Dob)

DUARTE, J.

61 *Variations on a Catalan Folk Song*, Op. 25 (Nov)

EASTWOOD, T.

62 *Ballade-Fantasy* (Fab; Bream)

FRICKER, P. R.

63 *Paseo* (Fab; Bream)

GERHARD, R.

64 *Fantasia for Guitar* (Mills)

MAGHINI, R.

65 *Umbra* (Berb)

MARTIN, F.

66 *Prélude AND Gigue* from *Quatre pièces brèves* (Uni; Scheit)

MORGAN, D.

67 *First Movement* from *Lyric Suite* (CMC)
68 *Third Movement* from *Lyric Suite* (CMC)

OBRAVSKA, J.

69 *Hommage à Béla Bartók* (Esch)

OHANA, M.

70 *Tiento* (Bill)
71 *20 Avril (Planh)*, No. 4 from *Si le jour paraît* (Bill)

ORBON, J.

72 *Preludio y danza* (FC; de la Torre)

SANTORSOLA, G.

73 *Vals romantico* (Berb; Gilardino)

SOMERS, H.

74 *Prelude, Scherzo AND Finale* from *Sonata for Guitar* (Cav)

TOROK, A.

75 *The Herdsmen*, No. 1 from *3 Sonatas* (CMC)
76 *Doux Sonate*, No. 2 from *3 Sonatas* (CMC)

STUDIES

Candidates must be prepared to play TWO studies of contrasting nature by different composers from the following list:

BARRIOS MANGORÉ, A.

77 *Estudio* from *Guitar Works*, Vol. 2, No. 6 (Belw; Stover)
78 *Estudio* from *Guitar Works*, Vol. 3, No. 13 (Belw; Stover)

COSTE, N.

79 *Twenty-five Études*, No. 19 in GA
80 *Twenty-five Études*, No. 21 in GA
81 *Twenty-five Études*, No. 22 in GA

DODGSON, S. and H. QUINE

82 *Studies for Guitar*, Vol. 1, No. 10 (Ric)
83 *Studies for Guitar*, Vol. 2, No. 11 (Ric)
84 *Studies for Guitar*, Vol. 2, No. 13 (Ric)
85 *Studies for Guitar*, Vol. 2, No. 20 (Ric)

GIULIANI, M.

86 *Studi per chitarra, No. 78* (SZ; Chiesa)

LAGOYA, A.

87 *Six Études, No. 3* (Esch)
88 *Six Études, No. 4* (Esch)
89 *Six Études, No. 5* (Esch)

PRESTI, I.

90 *Six Études, No. 6* (Esch)

PUJOL, E.

91 *Ondinas* (Ric)

SAGRERAS, J.

92 *El colibrí* (Ric) (M.M. ♩ = 144)

SOR, F.

93 *Twenty Studies, No. 12* (Marks; Segovia)
94 *Twenty Studies, No. 18* (Marks; Segovia)
95 *Twenty Studies, No. 20* (Marks; Segovia)

VILLA-LOBOS, H.

96 *Douze études, No. 2* (Esch)
97 *Douze études, No. 3* (Esch)
98 *Douze études, No. 5* (Esch)
99 *Douze études, No. 7* (Esch)
100 *Douze études, No. 9* (Esch)
101 *Douze études, No. 10* (Esch)
102 *Douze études, No. 12* (Esch)

TECHNICAL REQUIREMENTS

In preparing for the technical portion of the examination, Candidates should consult the *Royal Conservatory of Music Guitar Series: Scales and Arpeggios Album* (Oakville: Frederick Harris, 1990).

SCALES M.M. ♩ = 120

The Candidate must be prepared to play the following scales in triplet eighth notes and sixteenth notes, ascending and descending. The scales should be fingered *i m, m a, i a,* and any *i m a* combination of the Candidate's choosing and played with free strokes and rest strokes. **Scales are NOT to be fingered as first position, open-string scales.** Follow each scale with a I-IV-V-I cadence in a four-note form. See Technical Requirements Examples, p. 51.

Major . . . . all keys—2 and 3 octaves
where possible

Harmonic Minor . . . . . . all keys—2 and 3 octaves
where possible

Melodic Minor . . . . all keys—2 and 3 octaves
where possible

Chromatic . . . . starting on A—3 octaves

SLUR SCALES M.M. ♩ = 144

Ascending and descending, compound triplet slurs.

Major . . . . C, F—2 octaves

REPEATED-NOTE SCALES

Ascending and descending in triplets and quadruplets (M.M. ♩ = 120); in quintuplets and sextuplets (M.M. ♩ = 80), to be fingered *i m, m a, i a,* and any *i m a* combination; rest strokes throughout.

Major . . . . all keys—2 octaves

Harmonic Minor . . . . . . all keys—2 octaves

Melodic Minor . . . . . . all keys—2 octaves

SCALES IN THIRDS M.M. ♩ = 104

Ascending and descending solid form in eighth notes, broken form in sixteenths.

Major . . . . F—2 octaves

Harmonic Minor . . . . . . D—2 octaves

SCALES IN SIXTHS M.M. ♩ = 104

Ascending and descending solid form in eighth notes, broken form in sixteenths.

Major . . . . F—2 octaves

Harmonic Minor . . . . . . D—2 octaves

CHORDAL SCALES M.M. ♩ = 88

Ascending and descending solid form in eighth notes, broken form in triplet sixteenths.

Major . . . . F—2 octaves

Harmonic Minor . . . . . . D—2 octaves

EAR TESTS

A. **INTERVALS**

The Candidate will be required:

1. to sing or hum any of the following intervals after the first note has been played ONCE by the examiner;

OR (at the choice of the Candidate)

2. to identify any of the following intervals after each has been played ONCE in broken form by the examiner:

All intervals within the octave Above and Below a given note.

46

B. **MELODY PLAYBACK**

The Candidate will be required to play back the lower voice of a two-part phrase in a major key, after the examiner has:

1. named the key;

2. played the tonic chord ONCE; and

3. played the phrase TWICE.

Melody Example

C. **CHORDS**

The Candidate will be required to identify:

A. the quality (Major or Minor), and inversion (first inversion, second inversion or root position) of any major or minor four-note common chord in root position or first inversion; AND

B. the type (four-note common chord, dominant 7th or diminished 7th) of any four-note common chord, dominant or diminished 7th chord in root position when the chord is played ONCE by the examiner in solid form and in close position.

D. **CADENCES**

The Candidate will be required to identify by name or symbols any of the following cadences after the examiner has played the tonic chord ONCE, and then has TWICE played a short phrase in a major or minor key containing up to three cadences.

Perfect (Authentic or V-I), Imperfect (I-V), Deceptive (V-VI) and Plagal (IV-I).

Cadence Example

SIGHT READING

The Candidate will be required:

A. to play at sight given passages of music in contrasting styles; AND

B. to clap or tap the rhythm of a melody in 2/4 or 3/4 time. In order to achieve full marks, the Candidate must maintain a steady pace and metrical accentuation. The sight reading example indicates the approximate degree of difficulty of the melody.

Sight Reading Example

THEORY CO-REQUISITES

Grade 2 Rudiments

Grade 4 Harmony or Introductory Keyboard Harmony

Grade 3 History

Grade 4 History

SUPPLEMENTAL EXAMINATIONS

Please see p. 11.

PERFORMER'S ARCT

REPERTOIRE

Please note that the completion of all requirements, including theory co-requisites, for the Grade 10 certificate is a pre-requisite for the ARCT examination. Candidates must have achieved a minimum of 70 percent in each section of the Grade 10 practical examination. For additional information on up-grading a Candidate's Grade 10 status, please refer to Supplemental Examinations, p. 11. ARCT applications from Candidates who have failed to meet these requirements will not be accepted.

Candidates may qualify for Associateship of the Royal Conservatory of Music as either Performer or Teacher.

In order to obtain the ARCT Diploma, all theory co-requisites must be completed within FIVE years following the initial practical examination.

A high standard of performance is essential in this examination. The artistic balance of the lists presented is considered in the final assessment.

Memorization is compulsory. Candidates not playing from memory will receive comments only from the examiner's report. No marks will be awarded for any piece played with the music.

Ear tests and sight reading are not required for this examination.

A maximum of 70 minutes is allowed for the performance of six pieces, one from each of Lists A, B, C, D, and E. The pieces should be timed exactly, as the examiner will stop the performance if it exceeds the prescribed time limit.

Each numbered item represents one selection for examination purposes.

LIST A

BACH, J.S.

1   *Chaconne* from *Violin Partita in D Minor*, BWV 1004
2   *Prelude* AND *Fugue* from *Lute Suite No. 2 in C Minor*, BWV 997
3   *Prelude, Bourrée* AND *Gigue* from *Lute Suite No. 4 in E Major*, BWV 1006a
4   *Prelude, Fugue and Allegro for Lute in E-flat Major*, BWV 998

WEISS, S.L.

5   Any THREE Movements from *Suite No. 3* in *Intavolatura di liuto*, Vol. 1 (SZ; Chiesa)
6   *Allemande, Courante* AND *Angloise* from *Suite No. 14* in *Intavolatura di liuto*, Vol. 1 (SZ; Chiesa)

LIST B

GIULIANI, M.

7   *Grande ouverture*, Op. 61
8   *Sonata eroica*, Op. 150

PAGANINI, N.

9   *First* AND *Third Movements* from *Grand sonata*

SOR, F.

10 *Andante largo* AND *Allegro non troppo* from *Second Sonata*, Op. 25
11 *Gran solo*, Op. 14
12 *Variaciones sobre un tema de Paisiello*, Op. 16

LIST C

CASTELNUOVO-TEDESCO, M.

13 Any THREE Movements from *Sonata* in GA
14 *Capriccio diabolico* (Ric)

HARRIS, A.

15 *Variations and Fugue on a Theme of Handel* in GA

MANEN, J.

16 *Fantasia-Sonata* in GA

PONCE, M.

17 *First, Third* AND *Fourth Movements* from *Sonata No. 1* (Peer; Ramos)
18 *Thème varié et finale* in GA
19 *First* AND *Fourth Movements* from *Sonata romantica* in GA
20 *First* AND *Third Movements* from *Sonata III* in GA (Segovia)

RODRIGO, J.

21 *Invocation et danse* (EFM; Diaz)
22 Any TWO Movements from *Elogio de la guitarra* (Berb; Gilardino)
23 *First* AND *Third* Movements from *Sonata giocosa* (Ches)

LIST D

ARNOLD, M.

24 Any TWO of *Prelude, Scherzo, Fughetta, March* from *Fantasy for Guitar*, Op. 107 (Fab; Bream)

BROUWER, L.

25 *Tarantos* (Esch)

BRITTEN, B.

26 *Nocturnal*, Op. 70 (Fab; Bream)

CARTER, E.

27 *Changes* (Boo)

DODGSON, S.

28 *First, Second* AND *Fourth Movements* from *Partita* (Ox)
29 *Fantasy-Divisions* (Berb)

48

HENZE, H.W.

30 Any TWO Movements of *First Sonata* from *Royal Winter Music* in GA
31 Any TWO Movements of *Second Sonata* from *Royal Winter Music* in GA
32 *Drei Tentos* (Scho)

HÉTU, J.

33 *Prelude, Ballade AND Finale* from *Suite*, Op. 41 (Dob)

JAMIESON, D.

34 *Elegy* (Berb)
35 *First Movement* from *Sonata for Guitar* (CMC)

OHANA, M.

36 *Jeu des quatre vents* from *Si le jour paraît*, No. VI (Bill)

PETRASSI, G.

37 *Nunc* (SZ; Gangi)
38 *Suoni notturni* (Ric; Abloniz)

RAK, S.

39 *The Last Disco* (MNS)
40 *Voces de profundis* (MNS)
41 *The Sun* (MNS)

RAWSTHORNE, A.

42 *Elegy* (Ox; Bream)

SANTORSOLA, G.

43 Any TWO Movements from *Cuatro tientos* (B; Gilardino)

SCHAFER, M.

44 *Le Cri de Merlin* (CMC)

TAKEMITSU, T.

45 Any TWO Movements from *Folios* (Sal)

TIPPETT, M.

46 *First AND Third Movements* from *The Blue Guitar* (Scho)
47 *Second AND Third Movements* from *The Blue Guitar* (Scho)

WALTON, W.

48 *Five Bagatelles* (Ox; Bream), *Nos. 1, 3 AND 5*

LIST E

CASTELNUOVO-TEDESCO, M.

49 *First Movement* from *Concerto No. 1 in D*, Op. 99 in GA
50 *Third Movement* from *Concerto No. 1 in D*, Op. 99 in GA

GIULIANI, M.

51 *First Movement* from *Concerto*, Op. 30 (SZ)

RODRIGO, J.

52 *First Movement* from *Concierto de Aranjuez* (Belw) (Assoc)

VILLA-LOBOS, H.

53 *First Movement AND Cadenza* from *Concerto for Guitar* (Esch)
N.B. Candidates must provide their own accompanists; those failing to do so will not be examined.

THEORY CO-REQUISITES

Grade 4 Counterpoint

Grade 5 Harmony or Advanced Keyboard Harmony

Grade 5 Analysis

Grade 5 History

SUPPLEMENTAL EXAMINATIONS

Supplemental examinations are not available for the Performer's ARCT Diploma. Candidates who fail to obtain 70 percent of the total mark must re-apply for the entire examination.

TEACHER'S ARCT

REPERTOIRE

Please note that the completion of all requirements, including theory co-requisites, for the Grade 10 certificate is a pre-requisite for the ARCT examination. Candidates must have achieved a minimum of 70 percent in each section of the Grade 10 practical examination. For additional information on up-grading a Candidate's Grade 10 status, please refer to Supplemental Examinations, p. 11. ARCT applications from Candidates who have failed to meet these requirements will not be accepted.

Candidates may qualify for Associateship of the Royal Conservatory of Music as either Performer or Teacher.

In order to obtain the ARCT Diploma, all theory co-requisites must be completed within FIVE years following the initial practical examination.

The Teacher's ARCT Diploma will be awarded only to candidates 18 years of age or older.

Memorization is encouraged but not compulsory for the Teacher's Associateship examination. A high standard of performance is required.

Candidates must be prepared to perform TWO pieces, one from the Performer's ARCT, List B, and ONE from the Performer's ARCT, List C OR List D. Each numbered item represents one selection for examination purposes.

TECHNICAL REQUIREMENTS

In preparing for the technical portion of the examination, Candidates should consult the *Royal Conservatory of Music Guitar Series: Scales and Arpeggios Album* (Oakville: Frederick Harris, 1990).

SCALES M.M. ♩ = 120

The Candidate must be prepared to play the following scales in triplet eighth notes and sixteenth notes, ascending and descending. The scales should be fingered *i m*, *m a*, *i a*, and any *i m a* combination of the Candidate's choosing, and played with free strokes and rest strokes. **Scales are NOT to be fingered as first position, open-string scales.** Follow each scale with a I-IV-V-I cadence in a four-note form. See Technical Requirements Examples, p. 51.

Major . . . . all keys—2 and 3 octaves
where possible

Harmonic Minor . . . . . . all keys—2 and 3 octaves
where possible

Melodic Minor . . . . all keys—2 and 3 octaves
where possible

Chromatic . . . . starting on A—3 octaves

SLUR SCALES M.M. ♩ = 144

Ascending and descending, compound triplet slurs.

Major . . . . C, F—2 octaves

REPEATED-NOTE SCALES

Ascending and descending in triplets and quadruplets (M.M. ♩ = 120); in quintuplets and sextuplets (M.M. ♩ = 80), to be fingered *i m*, *m a*, *i a*, and any *i m a* combination; rest strokes throughout.

Major . . . . all keys—2 octaves

Harmonic Minor . . . . . . all keys—2 octaves

Melodic Minor . . . . all keys—2 octaves

SCALES IN THIRDS M.M. ♩ = 104

Ascending and descending solid form in eighth notes, broken form in sixteenths.

Major . . . . F—2 octaves

Harmonic Minor . . . . . . D—2 octaves

SCALES IN SIXTHS M.M. ♩ = 104

Ascending and descending solid form in eighth notes, broken form in sixteenths.

Major . . . . F—2 octaves

Harmonic Minor . . . . . . D—2 octaves

CHORDAL SCALES M.M. ♩ = 88

Ascending and descending solid form in eighth notes, broken form in triplet sixteenths.

Major . . . . F—2 octaves

Harmonic Minor . . . . . . D—2 octaves

EAR TESTS

A. METER

The Candidate may be required to identify the time signatures of given four-bar passages in 2/4, 3/4, 6/8 or 9/8 after each has been played ONCE by the examiner.

B. INTERVALS

The Candidate will be required:

1. to sing or hum any of the following intervals after the first note has been played ONCE by the examiner;

OR (at the choice of the Candidate)

2. to identify any of the following intervals after each has been played ONCE in broken form by the examiner:

All intervals within a Major 9th Above, and within an octave Below, a given note.

C. MELODY PLAYBACK

The Candidate will be required to play back both voices of a two-part phrase in a major key, after the examiner has:

1. named the key;

2. played the tonic chord ONCE; and

3. played the phrase TWICE.

Melody Example

D. CHORDS

The Candidate will be required to identify, using symbols (e.g., I, IV, V, I), chords in root position employed in a

50

four-bar phrase in a major key, beginning on the tonic. A cadential six-four may be used in the final cadence.

The examiner will play the tonic chord ONCE and then play the phrase TWICE in a slow to moderate tempo. During the second playing, the Candidate will name every chord in succession after each chord has been played by the examiner.

Chords Example

SIGHT READING

The Candidate will be required:

A. to play a short passage equal in difficulty to a Grade 9 piece; AND

B. to play at sight a given passage of music equal in difficulty to a Grade 3 piece, demonstrating its musical features; AND

C. to clap or tap the rhythm of a melody. In order to achieve full marks, the Candidate must maintain a steady pace and metrical accentuation. The sight reading example indicates the approximate degree of difficulty of the melody.

Sight Reading Example

VIVA VOCE

A. PEDAGOGICAL PRINCIPLES

Candidates will be examined orally on the principles of guitar playing, including position, condition, and action of the fingers, hands and arms; control and evenness of touch; tone production, phrasing, expression, and dynamics; the uses and functions of the nail, nail shaping, and repair; a practical knowledge of junior teaching materials and methodologies; a knowledge of basic technical exercises together with demonstrations if requested; the teaching of ear training and sight reading; an understanding of style appropriate to major composers and their musical and historical periods.

B. APPLIED PEDAGOGY

1. Teaching Repertoire

Candidates must be prepared to perform the following pieces, from which the examiners will choose a representative sampling, and to discuss the various teaching issues which arise from them, including details of style and interpretation:

THREE pieces from EACH of Grades 3 to 6, composed of a List A, B and C (where possible) piece from the current graded Syllabus lists; AND

FOUR pieces from each of Grades 7 and 8, with ONE piece selected from each of Lists A, B, C and D.

2. Detection of Errors and Demonstration Lesson

The examiners will select at least ONE piece from the graded repertoire presented by the Candidate. The Candidate must be prepared to detect any errors introduced by the examiners (time-values, rhythm, phrasing, interpretation, etc.), to suggest possible causes, and to provide solutions and practice methods for correcting these errors.

3. Knowledge of Classical Methods

The Candidate is expected to have a thorough knowledge of the classical guitar method books written by the following authors: Shearer, Noad, Duncan, Pujol, Sealy and Trotter, Henze, Carlevaro, Carcassi and Sor.

TEACHER'S WRITTEN PAPER (3 hours)

Seventy percent (70%) of the total mark of the Teacher's Written Examination (a MINIMUM Honours standing) is required for a Pass. No certificate is awarded for this paper.

Candidates must be prepared to answer questions in the following areas:

1. the history and development of the guitar and the stylistic characteristics of composers of guitar music, including Canadian composers. This may also include commentary on the realization of simple ornamentation relevant to guitar literature;

2. issues likely to arise in teaching, such as time and rhythm, part-playing, slurs, the correction of technical faults, development of basic technique, rubato, phrasing, playing expressively, methods of and reasons for memorization, sight reading, and ear training;

3. elementary psychology of music teaching; and

4. teaching materials of all styles for guitar students at all levels from beginners through Grade 8, including compositions, basic technique-building exercises, and studies.

Candidates must also be prepared to transcribe and edit for the guitar an excerpt from a piano score or Renaissance lute tablature of intermediate difficulty. Fingering, phrasing, dynamics, expression marks, and simple ornamentation should be added where necessary. The title and tempo of the excerpt will be given. The transcription must be playable. See p. 54 for a list of textbooks.

THEORY CO-REQUISITES

Grade 4 Counterpoint

Grade 5 Harmony or Advanced Keyboard Harmony

Grade 5 Analysis

Grade 5 History

ARCT Teacher's Written Examination

SUPPLEMENTAL EXAMINATIONS

Please see p. 11.

TECHNICAL REQUIREMENTS

TECHNICAL REQUIREMENTS EXAMPLES

Students should consult the *Royal Conservatory of Music Guitar Series: Scales and Arpeggios Album* (Oakville: Frederick Harris, 1990).

CADENCES

SLUR SCALES
Single Slurs
Compound Triplet Slurs

REPEATED-NOTE SCALES
In Sixteenth Notes
In Triplet Eighth Notes
In Quintuplets
In Sextuplets

SCALES IN THIRDS
In Solid Form
In Broken Form

SCALES IN SIXTHS
In Solid Form
In Broken Form

CHORDAL SCALE PATTERN
In Solid Form
In Broken Form

Please refer to the Theory Syllabus for detailed information on examination applications, policies, regulations and publications.

Theory examinations are given in the following subjects: Rudiments; Harmony, Counterpoint and Analysis; Music History; and Musicianship.

RUDIMENTS

PRELIMINARY RUDIMENTS

Elements of music for the beginner. One-hour examination.

GRADE 1 RUDIMENTS

A continuation of Preliminary Rudiments for students with more music reading experience. Two-hour examination.

GRADE 2 RUDIMENTS

Preliminary and Grade 1 Rudiments with the addition of foundation material necessary to the study of harmony. Two-hour examination.

HARMONY, COUNTERPOINT & ANALYSIS

GRADE 3 HARMONY

The fundamentals of four-part writing and melodic composition in major keys; harmonic and structural analysis in major and minor keys. Familiarity with material of Grade 2 Rudiments is strongly advised. Three-hour examination.

INTRODUCTORY KEYBOARD HARMONY

The material of Grade 3 Harmony at the keyboard. Examination may be substituted for Grade 3 Harmony in fulfillment of certificate requirements.

GRADE 4 HARMONY

Intermediate four-part writing and melodic composition in major and minor keys; modulation. Harmonic and structural analysis; musical forms. Completion of Grade 3 Harmony is strongly advised. Three-hour examination.

INTERMEDIATE KEYBOARD HARMONY

The material of Grade 4 Harmony at the keyboard. Examination may be substituted for Grade 4 Harmony in fulfillment of certificate requirements.

GRADE 4 COUNTERPOINT

Simple two-part counterpoint in Baroque style; invertible counterpoint at the octave and the fifteenth. Completion of Grade 3 and Grade 4 Harmony is strongly advised. Three-hour examination.

GRADE 5 HARMONY
(HARMONY AND COUNTERPOINT)

Advanced harmonic and intermediate contrapuntal techniques (for two voices). Completion of Grades 3 and 4 Harmony and Grade 4 Counterpoint is strongly advised. Three-hour examination.

ADVANCED KEYBOARD HARMONY

The material of Grade 5 Harmony and Counterpoint at the keyboard. Examination may be substituted for Grade 5 Harmony in fulfillment of certificate requirements.

GRADE 5 ANALYSIS

Advanced harmonic and structural analysis (musical forms) based on the material of Grades 3, 4 and 5 Harmony and Counterpoint. Three-hour examination.

MUSIC HISTORY

GRADE 3 HISTORY

Styles, composers and music of the Romantic period. Three-hour examination.

GRADE 4 HISTORY

Styles, composers and music of the Medieval, Renaissance, Baroque, Rococo and Classical periods. Three-hour examination.

GRADE 5 HISTORY

Styles, composers and music of the 20th century; Canadian music. Three-hour examination.

MUSICIANSHIP

These examinations may be substituted for the Ear Tests in instrumental examinations at the option of the Candidate.

JUNIOR MUSICIANSHIP

Singing and/or identification of scales, intervals and chords; aural analysis of simple harmonic progressions, singing back and sight singing of simple rhythms and melodies. To be used with Grade 8 practical examinations.

INTERMEDIATE MUSICIANSHIP

Singing and/or identification of scales, intervals and chords; aural analysis of harmonic progressions; singing back and sight singing of rhythms and melodies. To be used with Grade 9 practical examinations.

Singing and/or identifications of scales, intervals and chords; aural analysis of harmonic progressions to the Grade 4 Harmony level; singing back and sight singing of rhythms and melodies. To be used with Grade 10 practical examinations.

COMPLETION DEADLINES

All theory co-requisites must be completed within five years following the sessions of the practical examination to which they apply. Extensions will not be granted.

CLASSIFICATION OF THEORY EXAMINATION MARKS

The following marking categories apply to the Theory examinations:

First Class Honours 80-100
Honours 70-79
Pass 60-69

TEXTBOOKS

For a complete list of recommended textbooks, please consult the Theory Syllabus.

Past RCM examination papers are available from the RCM Music Store.

PRE- AND CO-REQUISITES

Commencing at the Grade 5 level, Candidates for RCM certificates must complete prescribed theory examinations in addition to practical examinations. The following table indicates co-requisite (C) and pre-requisite (P) theory requirements from Grade 5 through ARCT.

Grade 5	Preliminary Rudiments (C)
Grade 6	Grade 1 Rudiments (C)
Grade 7	Grade 2 Rudiments (C)
Grade 8	Grade 2 Rudiments (C)
Grade 9	Grade 2 Rudiments (C), Grade 3 Harmony (C), Grade 3 History (C)
Grade 10	Grade 2 Rudiments (C), Grade 4 Harmony (C), Grades 3 and 4 History (C)
ARCT	Grade 2 Rudiments (P), Grade 4 Harmony (P), Grade 5 Harmony (C), Grades 3 and 4 History (P), Grade 5 History (C), Grade 4 Counterpoint (C), Grade 5 Analysis (C)

PART IV

RECOMMENDED PUBLICATIONS

The following editions are produced by the RCM and are published by The Frederick Harris Music Co., Limited, or by the RCM.

Royal Conservatory of Music. *Guitar Series: Repertoire and Studies Album.* 8 vols. Grades 1 through 8. Oakville: Frederick Harris, 1989-90.

Royal Conservatory of Music. *Guitar Series: Scales and Arpeggios Album.* Oakville: Frederick Harris, 1990.

Royal Conservatory of Music. *Cassette Tapes to accompany the Guitar Series.* 8 vols. Recorded by the Faculty of the Royal Conservatory of Music. Oakville: Frederick Harris, 1990.

Royal Conservatory of Music. *Guitar Syllabus.* Oakville: Frederick Harris, 1990.

Royal Conservatory of Music. *Theory Syllabus.* Oakville: Frederick Harris, 1989.

Royal Conservatory of Music. *Individual Examination Papers from Past Sessions.* Toronto: Royal Conservatory of Music, various years. Order through the RCM Music Store. Minimum of three papers per mail order.

Royal Conservatory of Music. *Bundled Examination Papers; Set No. 1: Preliminary, Grade 1 and Grade 2 Rudiments; Set No. 2: Harmony 3, 4 and 5; History 3, 4 and 5; Counterpoint 4 and Analysis 5.*

Sets of 5 papers from the same grade, session and subject are available for sale from the RCM Music Store. Include with each order the quantity, set number (if applicable), grade, subject and quantity, as well as year and session (summer or winter).

RCM Dialogue (formerly the *Examination Newsletter*). The *RCM Dialogue* is mailed four times per year to teachers who have submitted students for examinations. Additional copies are available from music stores, RCM Co-ordinators or Representatives and the Examination Department.

The Academic Year. Published annually in the summer. A complete guide to RCM programs and faculty.

ARCT TEACHER'S EXAMINATIONS

Royal Conservatory of Music. *Questions and Answers Illustrative of the Viva Voce Examination.* Toronto: Royal Conservatory of Music, 1988. Specify the Piano or Voice edition when ordering.

Individual ARCT Teacher's Written Examination papers are available on request from the RCM Music Store.

PUBLICATIONS OF GENERAL INTEREST

Music Magazine/RCM Bulletin. Published since 1987 as part of *Music Magazine*, the *RCM Bulletin* provides up-to-date information on RCM activities. Five issues per year. Subscriptions are available from *Music Magazine*, P.O. Box 96, Station R, Toronto, Ontario M4G 9Z9.

To obtain any of the above publications, contact your local music store or address mail orders to Royal Conservatory Music Store, 273 Bloor St., West, Toronto, Ontario M5S 1W2. Please do not pre-pay by cheque. Payment may be made by VISA, MASTERCARD (include card number and expiry date) or by cheque upon receipt of our invoice. Members of the RCM Alumni Association are entitled to a 10% discount upon request. Please indicate Branch Affiliation when ordering.

TEXTBOOKS

The following texts have been found useful for reference, teaching and examination preparation. No single text is necessarily complete for examination purposes.

GENERAL REFERENCE

Arnold, D., ed. *New Oxford Companion to Music.* New York: Oxford University Press, 1983.

Hindley, G., ed. *Larousse Encyclopedia of Music.* London: Hamlyn, 1971.

Irvine, D., and R.G. Condie. *How to Prepare for and Take a Practical Examination.* Oakville: Frederick Harris, 1984.

Kallmann, H., G. Potvin, and K. Winters, eds. *Encyclopedia of Music in Canada.* Toronto: University of Toronto Press, 1981.

Randel, D., ed. *New Harvard Dictionary of Music.* Cambridge, Mass.: Harvard University Press, 1987.

Randel, D., ed. *Concise Harvard Dictionary of Music.* Cambridge, Mass.: Harvard University Press, 1978.

Sadie, S., ed. *The New Grove Dictionary of Music and Musicians.* 20 vols. London: Macmillan, 1980.

Scholes, P. *Concise Oxford Dictionary of Music.* London: Oxford University Press, 1979.

Scholes, P., ed. *Oxford Junior Companion to Music.* London: Oxford University Press, 1979.

SIGHT READING AND EAR TRAINING

Benedict, R. *Sight Reading for the Classical Guitar*. Levels 1 to 3, Levels 4 and 5. Miami: Belwin Mills.

Bennett, E., and H. Capp. *Sight Reading and Ear Tests*. 9 vols. Oakville: Frederick Harris, 1968-70.

Berlin, B. *Four Star Sight Reading*. 8 vols. Oakville: Frederick Harris, 1969-70.

Berlin, B., and A. Markow. *Ear Training for Practical Examinations. Melody Playback/Singback*. 4 vols. Oakville: Frederick Harris, 1986-88.

Berlin, B., and W. Mould. *Rhythmic Tests for Sight Reading*. Grades 8 to ARCT. Toronto: G. Thompson, 1969.

Hegyi, E. *Solfège according to the Kodály Concept*. Vol. 1. Kecskemét, Hungary: Zoltán Kodály Pedagogical Institute of Music, 1975. Vol. 2. Budapest: Editio Musica Budapest, 1979.

Hindemith, P. *Elementary Training for Musicians*. London: Schott, 1974.

Starer, R. *Rhythmic Training for Musicians*. Melville, New York: MCA, 1969.

Warburton, A.O. *Graded Aural Tests*. London: Longman, 1971.

PRACTISING & PERFORMING

Artzt, A. *The Art of Practicing*. Shaftsbury: Musical New Services, 1978.

Bellow, A. *The Illustrated History of the Guitar*. New York: Colombo, c. 1970.

Bluetens, S. *Method for the Renaissance Lute*. Menlo Park, Ca.: Instrumenta Antiqua, 1969.

Buck, P.L. *Psychology for Musicians*. London: Oxford University Press, 1949

Carlevaro, A. *School of Guitar: Exposition of Instrumental Theory*. London: Boosey & Hawkes, 1984.

Cortot, A. *Studies in Musical Interpretation*. London: Harrap, 1937.

Curwen, A.J. *Psychology Applied to Music Teaching*. London: Curwen, 1920.

Dart, T. *The Interpretation of Music*. London: Hutchinson, 1967.

Delamont, G. *Modern Harmonic Technique*. New York: Kendor, c. 1965.

Dolmetsch, A. *The Interpretation of the Music of the 17th and 18th Centuries*. London: Novello, 1946.

Donington, R. *The Interpretation of Early Music*. London: Faber & Faber, 1989.

Donington, R. *A Performer's Guide to Baroque Music*. London: Faber & Faber, 1973.

Duarte, J. *The Guitarist's Hands*. Australia: Universal, c. 1978.

Duarte, J. *The Bases of Classic Guitar Technique*. Borough Green: Novello, 1975.

Duncan, C. *The Art of Classical Guitar Playing*. Princeton: Summy-Birchard, c. 1980.

Emery, W. *Bach's Ornaments*. London: Novello, 1953.

Grunfeld, F.V. *The Art and Times of the Guitar*. New York: Macmillan, 1969.

Guitar Master Class: Technical Exercises by Famous Guitarists. Melville, N.Y.: Belwin Mills, c. 1980.

Hindemith, P. *Elementary Training for Musicians*. New York: Schott, 1949.

Jaques-Dalcroze, E. *Rhythm, Music and Education*. New York: Putman, 1921.

Lilienfeld, R., and B. Cimino. *The Guitarist's Harmony*. New York: Franco Colombo, 1965.

MacKinnon, L. *Music by Heart*. Westport, Conn.: Greenwood Press, 1981.

Matthay, T. *Musical Interpretation*. Boston: Boston Music, 1913.

Matthay, T. *On Memorizing*. London: Oxford, 1948.

Ryan, L.F. *The Natural Classical Guitar*. Englewood Cliffs, N.J.: Prentice-Hall, c. 1984.

Smith Brindle, R. *Serial Composition*. London: Oxford University Press, 1966.

Taylor, J. *Tone Production on the Classical Guitar*. London: Musical New Services, 1978.

ALBERTA

Calgary
Mrs. Margaret F. Brown
908 - 319 - 26th Ave. SW
Calgary, Alberta T2S 2T9

Edmonton
Mrs. Norma A. Robertson
5004 -124th St.
Edmonton, Alberta T6H 3T9
(403) 434-4002

Lethbridge
Mrs. Elda Jorgensen
1106 - 15th St. N.
Lethbridge, Alberta T1H 2Y6
(403) 328-3527

BRITISH COLUMBIA

New Westminster
Ms. Mary Fraser
6562 Elwell St.
Burnaby, British Columbia V5E 1J8

Vancouver
Mrs. Dianne Globe
4650 Garden Grove Dr.
Burnaby, British Columbia V5G 3V3
(604)434-0857

Victoria
Mrs. Kathleen Jennings
409 - 548 Dallas Rd
Victoria, British Columbia V8V 1B3
(604) 384-0175

MANITOBA

Winnipeg
Mrs. Marlene Pauls Laucht
165 Cordova St.
Winnipeg, Manitoba R3N 1A2
(204) 489-5912

NOVA SCOTIA

Halifax
Mr. Anton Los
Box 10, Site 14, R.R. #1
Eastern Passage
Halifax County, Nova Scotia B0J 1L0
(902) 465-1337

ONTARIO

Ottawa
Mrs. Mae Daly
R.R. #1
Wilson's Corners, P.Q. J0X 3J0
(819) 671-2349

QUEBEC

Montreal
Mrs. Rita M. Doucas
23 Rodney Ave.
Pointe Claire, P.Q. H9R 4L8
(514) 697-3561

SASKATCHEWAN

Regina
Mrs. Marjorie Templeton
5321 - 1st Ave.
Regina, Saskatchewan S4T 0A7
(306) 545-1378

Saskatoon
Mrs. Lorna Whelan
2280 - 424 Spadina Cres. E.
Saskatoon, Saskatchewan S7K 6X7
(306) 242-7353

OFFICERS

Principal's Office
Acting Principal   Gordon Kushner
Secretary to the Principal   Carole Chapman

Vice-Principal's Office
Vice-Principal   Robert E. Creech
Office Manager   Louise Yearwood
Records and Awards Officer   Lynn Slotkin
Ensemble & Choral Assistant   Pauline Lam
General Studies Coordinator   Mary Ann Ross
Ensembles, Instrumental
    & Vocal Studies Coordinator   John Barnum
Academic Development Consultant   G. Campbell Trowsdale
Theory and Children's
    Programs Coordinator   John Kruspe
Publications Consultant   Hugh McLean
Publications Assistant   Donald Anderson

Academic Chairmen
Theory   Maurice White
Speech and Drama   Sandra Cannon
Orchestral Instruments   Margot Onodera
Strings   Angelo Calcafuoco
Keyboard   Andrew Markow
Voice   Helen Simmie
Children's Programs   Spiro Kizas

Financial and Administrative Services
Manager   Hiie Galea
Administrative Consultant   George Hoskins
Manager, Accounting   Yvonne Ho
Information Systems Analyst   Robert Russell
Contracts & Records Assistant   Barbara Quan
Supervisor, Registration Desk   Lillian Carleton
Manager, Physical Plant   Michael Culbert
Manager, Music Store   Danny Bishop

Examination Department
Director   Daryl Irvine
Theory Examinations Coordinator   Wally Cochrane
Practical Examinations Supervisor   Margaret Dagens
Computer Operations Supervisor   Terry Payne
Examination Centres Coordinator   Mary-Ellen Béchard

Public Relations and Marketing
Coordinator   Andrew Stewart
Concerts and Public Events Officer   Dean Perry